I Can't
Sit Still

I Can't Sit Still

Educating and Affirming Inattentive and Hyperactive Children

Dorothy Davies Johnson, MD, FAAP

Suggestions for teachers, parents and other care providers of children to age 10

ETR ASSOCIATES
Santa Cruz, California
1992

ETR Associates (Education, Training and Research) is a nonprofit organization committed to fostering the health, well-being and cultural diversity of individuals, families, schools and communities. The publishing program of ETR Associates provides books and materials that empower young people and adults with the skills to make positive health choices. We invite health professionals to learn more about our high-quality resources and our training and research programs by contacting us at P.O. Box 1830, Santa Cruz, CA 95061-1830.

10 9 8 7 6 5

Printed in the United States of America

Illustrations by Marcia Quackenbush and JoAnna Fainberg
Design by Ann Smiley and Julia Chiapella

Library of Congress Cataloging-in-Publication Data

Johnson, Dorothy Davies
     I can't sit still : educating and affirming inattentive and hyperactive children : suggestions for teachers, parents and other care providers of children to age 10 / Dorothy Davies Johnson.
         p.   cm.
     Includes bibliographical references (p.).
     ISBN 1–56071–079–9
     1. Hyperactive children—Education. 2. Problem children—Education. 3. Self-respect in children. 4. Hyperactive children—Family relationships. I. Title.
     LC4711.J64   1992
     371.93—dc20   91–39464

Title No. 560

To Margaret Rauch Davies, my mother and my friend.

—D.D.J.

Contents

Acknowledgments   ix

Introduction   1

What Does ADHD Mean?   2
What Does ADHD Have to Do with Self-Esteem?   2
Can Anything Help?   3

Chapter 1.   Special Children: A Directional Difficulty and Hyperspeed   5
A Bike with ADHD   7
But What About People?   9
The Good and Bad of ADHD   11
Other Special Challenges   13
What the Problems Look Like   15
Making It Easier   17

Chapter 2.   Understanding What's Different: Diagnosing and Demystifying   19
What Else Could It Be?   20
Causes of Attention Problems   21
Symptoms at School   22
Getting Help   25
A Word to Families   27
How a Diagnosis Helps   28

Chapter 3.   Tools of the Trade: Strategies for Coping with ADHD   29
Adaptations   32
Behavior Management Strategies   33
Bonus Points Sample Chart   38
Cognitive-Behavioral Training   39
Drug Therapy   44

Chapter 4.   The Self-Esteem Connection   50
Esteem Kid   52
Feeling Valued   53
Feeling in Control   56
Feeling Capable   58
Protection from Embarrassment   59

Chapter 5.   Enjoying the Trip: Protecting Feelings and Managing
              Anger   64
              Why Is Everybody Shouting?   66
              Anger Risk Insurance   67
                  Anger Insurance House   68
              Rest and Relaxation   69
              Feeling Vents   70
              Protection   70
              Insulation   73
              Laughter   74
              Communication   75
                  Y-Man   76
              Action Plans   81

Chapter 6.   ROADS to Classroom Success   93
              Restructuring   96
              Organization   102
                  Sample Assignment Sheet   104
              Attention   108
              Dealing with Other Difficulties   117
              Share the Load   125

Chapter 7.   The Home Front   127
              Behavior Management Strategies at Home   128
              Daily Challenges   133
              Family Matters   141
              Between Home and School   146
              Life's Pleasures   149

Appendix A.   Studies on Self-Esteem and ADHD   153

Appendix B.   What Else Could It Be?   155

Appendix C.   The School Assessment   159

Appendix D.   The Yale Children's Inventory   163

Appendix E.   Diagnostic Criteria   169

Appendix F   More About Medication   171

Suggested Readings   175

References   177

Acknowledgments

It seems that this book began a very long time ago, even before I was a parent. It has evolved from years of dialogue and shared problem solving as a pediatrician, as a consultant and as a parent. There are many people to thank—more than I can name—but here are some.

On the home front:

My husband, Henry, for accepting, exciting, calming, broadening, freeing, anchoring and loving me.

Our son, Charlie, for sharing the adventure, introducing me to new worlds and planting the first roses in our garden.

My mother, Margaret Davies, and my husband's parents, Helen and Henry Johnson, Sr., for giving patiently, persistently, lovingly.

Our teachers, ministers, youth leaders, friends, counselors and home helpers, who have been invaluably wise and giving parenting trainers and extenders.

Linda Bernstein, Rita Clark, Jeannie Stutzer, Bruce and Ginny Wallies, and Paul LaFranz, who have especially enjoyed, understood and believed in the exuberance.

On the professional side:

The children and parents who come to see me, who continue to be my teachers, and especially Zak Bourke, who first showed me about crashes.

The multiple teachers, nurses, guidance counselors, psychologists and administrators of San Diego Unified and San Diego County schools, whose experience, examples, questions and comments have given practicality to concept.

Pauline Neuman, secretary, manager, super-mom, for nurturing and coordinating "our" families and me.

Mark Katz, Terri Fong, Ken Heying, Roland Rotz, Martha Hillyard, Sharon Foster and Clare Jones, for sharing their breadth of knowledge, their tremendous experience and their creative, caring energies.

Susie Horn, Judy Beck, Connie Strohbehn and Marc Lewkowicz— visionaries with soul who make good things happen.

Doctors Mel Levine, Bill Coleman and Jeff Black and Professor Jerry Ammer, for their uncommon insights and support during my professional retooling.

Chris Paré, Bev Kilman, Linda Charles, Gordon Amundson, Patrick Buckus, Kathy Blake and Doctors Doris Trauner, Phil Nader, Dennis Cantwell and Barry Garfinkel, for their contributions to the understandings and the opportunities.

And, most immediately, to ETR editors Kathleen Middleton and Netha Thacker and production staff Sarah Lamb and Suzanne Schrag, whose clarity and skill have helped transform information into communication and made the task of writing a joy.

Introduction

This book is for and about children who are Astonishingly Divergent, Huggable and Dynamic. Astonishingly divergent, they surprise and amaze one as their thoughts and actions head off in unexpected and creative directions. Huggable and enjoyable, they are anchored and nourished by backrubs, hands to hold, family hugs, as well as encouraging words and appreciative laughter. Dynamic, one of these children may have enough energy for twenty others.

This book refers to children with ADHD, now officially known as *Attention Deficit Hyperactivity Disorder*. In one year or ten years, the official name will change, but some children will continue to be ADHD— *astonishingly divergent, huggable* and *dynamic*. They will continue to have trouble keeping their attention aimed in the right direction and to struggle with speed spurts, going too fast or too slowly.

Let yourself be astonished not only by their challenges but by their gifts, not only by their demands but by your ability to make a difference for them. Understand what divergent means. Free yourself to enjoy and nurture them. And put on your running shoes—these dynamic children can't sit still for long.

What Does ADHD Mean?

Some children have an unusually difficult time concentrating, staying on task, following directions, reflecting, being calm, organizing their ideas and belongings, sitting still and being quiet. It's not because they don't try or because they have bad parents or teachers. It's because their brains' systems for letting them choose what to pay attention to and what to do aren't very effective.

These children have biological differences in the regulatory system of their brains which give them less-stable steering of their attention (attention deficit disorder) and less-reliable control over the pace at which they think and act (hyperactivity). These children are said to have ADHD, or attention deficit hyperactivity disorder.

What Does ADHD Have to Do with Self-Esteem?

Children with ADHD may start out as wonderfully enthusiastic children, but their difficulties can begin to make them feel incapable or "dumb." Sometimes they become very angry or sad or silly because of their frustrations. In turn, their difficulties can make the adults who care for them feel angry, helpless, frustrated and guilty.

All that frustration can lead to low self-esteem. Then all the wonderful qualities of these children—creativity, enthusiasm, goodwill, knowledge, talents and caring—can get lost. If self-esteem is lost, what started out as a challenge becomes a tragedy.

The purpose of this book is to help children, teachers, parents and other caregivers understand what ADHD is and isn't and to give them ways to communicate positively about it. The book also provides tools for dealing constructively with the special challenges of ADHD while protecting and fostering children's belief in themselves and enhancing their gifts. Parents and teachers, too, may gain renewed self-confidence as they more successfully assist these challenged children.

Can Anything Help?

Research has made clear that low self-esteem is a major problem in children with ADHD. However, it also indicates that a combination of educational, family and medical assistance can improve self-esteem and long-term outcome in children with ADHD symptoms. Adults who had ADHD as children have said that the most important thing contributing to their adult success was that someone—usually a parent or teacher—had believed in them.

Research has also found that mothers of children with ADHD tend to be depressed, have low self-esteem and be negative in their interactions with these children. When the child's symptoms improve on medication, the mother's depression lifts and she is able to offer more encouragement to the child.

Discussions with teachers suggest that their self-esteem, too, is affected by the challenges of ADHD. One teacher told me that she had awakened out of a nightmare in which she was trying unsuccessfully to help a boy in her class who has ADHD to find that, in her distress, she had been biting her knuckles in her sleep.

Teachers, school nurses, guidance counselors and principals, now aware of ADHD, are hungry for ways to help. They are asking for strategies for communicating with parents and affected students as well as strategies for classroom and playground management.

The strategies must be compatible with limited budgets and large classrooms of diverse students. If they are to enhance student self-esteem, these strategies cannot simply involve placing the child's desk alone, facing a wall.

School staff also need to be aware that many factors unrelated to ADHD can cause a child to be restless and distracted. These factors need other types of assistance. School staff need to know whom to call for assistance in diagnosing and treating these problems.

Staff need to understand what medication can and can't do and to feel comfortable in assisting the student for whom medication has been prescribed. Teachers also need information to share with parents who may be confused, defensive or pleading for assistance.

This book was written to give adults and children a non-threatening framework for thinking and communicating about the reality of the challenges of ADHD and for protecting and enhancing children's self-esteem as well as that of parents and teachers.

Chapter 1

Special Children:
A Directional Difficulty
and Hyperspeed

People are different. Some people are fast, and some people are slower, more careful and methodical. Some people think a long time before they decide which bracelet or baseball card to buy, and some buy the first one they see. Some people need to take medicine every day if their bodies don't make enough of something (like thyroid or insulin) or make too much of something (like histamine). Some people wear glasses and some don't.

What's more, people aren't the same every day. Some days we wake up feeling cheerful and everything seems great. Another day we may feel miserable because of a little headache, a restless sleep, an unkind word or a worry we didn't even know we had.

And we're different in different situations. Some things are very interesting—so interesting that we can spend a long time thinking about them and not get bored—while other things just don't turn us on.

This book is about dealing with differences—differences that are partly wonderful and partly very difficult. It's especially about a particular group of differences that are sometimes called ADD or ADHD.

I like to think of ADD as *A Directional Difficulty,* but its official name is *Attention Deficit Disorder.* I think of the *H* in ADHD as *Hyperspeed,* although its official name is *Hyperactivity.*

Having ADHD is special. To be special means to be different and unique. It's not necessarily good or bad. It makes some things easier and some things harder.

ADHD isn't the same for everyone, so when you're thinking about one particular child as you read this book, you'll find some things that fit and some things that don't. Those non-fits remind us that we're talking about children—wonderfully unique and different, whether they have black or blond hair, wear glasses or hearing aids, or collect lizards, baseball cards or dolls.

A Bike with ADHD

One way to think about ADHD is to imagine a bicycle that has hyperspeed and a directional difficulty. This wonderful bicycle is very strong and very light. It has a leather-covered seat, 21 speeds, cushioned handle bars, and custom color and trim chosen by the owner.

Imagine that a boy takes this brand new bicycle out for a ride and heads up a hill. As he goes up the hill he thinks, Wow! What a bike! He zips up the hill without even having to zig-zag. Then he goes to a large empty parking lot to ride around. The bike is fast, it coasts well, it's comfortable.

The boy might notice that he can't make the bike go exactly where he wants it to go, and it seems to be hard to get it to stop when he wants it to, but in the big parking lot that doesn't matter too much. He may wonder if he just hasn't learned how to ride this fancy bike or if something else is wrong.

He doesn't yet realize that the steering is loose. The wheel doesn't turn exactly when he turns the handle bars, so the bike doesn't go exactly where he thought he was going. The bike has a directional difficulty.

The brakes are loose too, so sometimes the boy goes fast when he'd meant to slow down. The bike has hyperspeed. Hyperspeed and a directional difficulty make the bike hard to ride, but you can't tell just by looking that there's anything wrong with the bike. Sometimes, the boy feels as if he just doesn't know how to ride the bike.

Imagine that the next weekend he goes biking along the bike path at the park with his parents. He keeps up with them going up the hills. But then the path begins to wind, and the bike keeps going off onto the grass because of its steering problem. And every time people cross the path in front of him, the boy has to jump off the bike or go into the grass to keep from hitting them. He's not sure what's going on.

What happens next? Maybe his mom or dad starts yelling at him. "Steer! Watch where you're going! Look out! Slow down! Stop!" Maybe the bike runs into a pothole and he falls. Even without a crash, he may become pretty upset.

He may feel angry at himself for not getting the bike to go where he wants it to go. He may get angry at the bike. He may get angry at his parents for yelling at him.

The boy and his parents don't know that the bike has loose steering and brakes; they just know that the boy can't seem to get it to go where he wants it to at the speed he wants it to go. Everyone feels annoyed.

Now imagine that someone at the park has seen this happen with other bikes. Maybe this person is a bike shop owner or someone who's had a bike with loose steering and brakes. He or she mentions to the boy's parents that they should check it out, because one out of every twenty of those special, custom-made bikes has this difficulty.

The family takes the bike to the bike shop, and the people at the shop confirm the problem. This excellent, custom-painted bike does have loose steering and loose brakes—a directional difficulty and hyperspeed.

Now what? This is a special dream bike. The boy knows there's no other bike as special as his. Now that he and his parents know what the problem is, everyone can stop feeling angry and just go get the tools needed to fix it.

Maybe they need a wrench or pliers or a screwdriver. If, even with good tools, the steering tends to keep getting loose, it might need to be tightened every day.

And maybe the boy needs to learn some special tricks for riding the bike on winding roads and down hills. Maybe he can use the gears to help him slow down when the brakes aren't working well.

Maybe the bike will work if he starts turning and braking a long time before he thinks he needs to. Maybe the family can find bike paths that don't have as many sharp turns.

The boy can enjoy going long distances and up steep hills on this bike; he can enjoy the comfortable seat and handle bars; and he can enjoy the bike's classy looks. He may even begin to feel proud that he is the one person who has learned how to ride this special and different bike.

But What About People?

OK. Enough about bikes. What does a bike have to do with this thing called ADHD in people?

Well, people steer themselves through each hour of every day. Choosing what to do and what to pay attention to are kinds of steering that our minds do all the time. Our steering system lets us concentrate on something for a long time, ignore sights or sounds that aren't important, and sit, walk, run or skip.

When we decide to wait to think about choices before we act, keep from saying a mean word that we thought about saying, or stop doing something because someone else asks us to, we're using our brakes. If we have trouble paying attention and stopping, we may have trouble doing what we choose to do. We may find that, as Dennis the Menace once said, "By the time I think about what I'm going to do, I already did it."

All of us have steering and braking problems some of the time. If we're tired or hungry or sick or worried, we may have more trouble paying attention and being careful.

But some people are like the boy with that special bike. The brain system that is supposed to steer and stop, to help them organize, concentrate, slow down and choose, doesn't do its job as well in those people as in others.

How do we know that the problem is actually in the brain's control system and not just due to poor parenting, inadequate education or an unwilling child?

The pattern of ADHD symptoms was first identified in the early 1900s among many people who had recovered from an epidemic of viral brain infection, or encephalitis. Similar symptoms have been observed after prenatal alcohol exposure, lead poisoning, or high speed car accidents which resulted in some degree of brain dysfunction.

Many children with ADHD have relatives with similar symptoms. Adopted children tend to resemble the families of their birth parents, not their adopted families, in regard to ADHD symptoms. These findings indicate that in these children ADHD is inherited rather than a response to parenting style.

Recent studies at the National Institutes of Mental Health demonstrate different brain function in people with inherited ADHD compared to those without symptoms of ADHD (Zametkin, 1990). The organizing, planning "prefrontal" area of the brain seems to be less active in people with ADHD.

Medications can make a big difference in impulse control and attentional focus in children with inherited ADHD. The most effective medications increase the activity of catecholamines, the chemicals of the brain's regulating system. This system works like a good radio tuner, allowing us to choose a major focus by screening out or increasing the impact of various nerve messages.

What's important to a child is knowing that the steering and braking system is a different part of the brain than the parts that make a person smart. Lots of people with ADHD are very smart. They may also have special talents. Sometimes the very fact that the brain isn't so organized about what it thinks about leads to wonderful creativity and inventiveness—the delightful surprises of wandering.

Sometimes the fact that these people are paying attention to so many things at once is very helpful. One boy saved his baby sister's life because he heard the noise when she fell into the pool and rescued her, even though he'd been in another part of the yard. If he'd been concentrating better on the game he was playing, his sister might not be alive.

Of the adults I know who have ADHD, one is a superb professional artist, several have their own inventive companies, one is a top executive in a development firm, and several are photographers. I especially like to think about photographers with ADHD. If they are looking all around, distracted by this and that, they are more likely to happen to see something special than the person who just concentrates on the path.

Their wandering attention allows them to capture those wonderful things others miss. And when photographers really need to concentrate, they go into a dark room and turn out all the lights, except for the red light on their work, so they have minimal distractions.

Other adults I know who have had ADHD are doctors and taxi drivers, traveling salesmen and lawyers, engineers, teachers and financial consultants. These successful adults came to believe in themselves, were able to choose careers that excite them (it's much easier to pay attention to something you love), and have learned coping strategies. For instance, an executive told me he does the necessary legal reading between 6:30 and 8:30 every morning so there are no distractions, and an engineer said he goes to team sessions during the day but does his detail work between 8:00 p.m. and midnight.

The Good and Bad of ADHD

What's good about ADHD? Children with ADHD are usually very divergent. They tend to think of and do lots of different things. They make interesting and unexpected connections and tend to be exciting and creative. They often cultivate the humor that comes from the ability to see things differently.

These children observe things most of us don't notice. They scan their world rapidly, although seldom in a sequential or systematic fashion. Their drawings tend to be of whole battles and whole arenas (audience and all), with multiple stick figures and squiggles rather than two detailed warriors or wrestlers.

The scanning tends to give these children a good "gestalt" sense of places they've been. The tendency to see the whole screen at once may give them an advantage in video games, where alertness to things coming from all directions is important for survival. If they don't have a learning disability, they tend to gather and remember a great deal of information, although it is not necessarily the information that others (such as teachers) think is most important.

These children's urge to move tends to make them excel in nonstop sports such as biking, swimming, tennis and soccer (when they're attentive enough to keep track of the ball and which goal is which). They have as strong a desire as any other child to please those around them, to do well, to be good.

But not everything is so easy. Students with ADHD have a hard time being convergent. It's hard for them to do or say or remember the exact one thing that someone else wants or needs of them.

They can be very fascinating and entertaining, and as adults they tend to do a lot of interesting things. But school tends to be an unfriendly environment for astonishingly divergent children because it requires a lot of convergent stuff.

Loose steering and brakes aren't too much of a problem in a big empty parking lot, but they can be a big problem on a narrow path. ADHD is much more of a problem where there are lots of things that have to be done according to someone else's guidance, such as getting ready for school and doing schoolwork.

Think about school. All day long, you have to do, say and remember exactly what the teacher asks of you. As a matter of fact, school is a job that most children with ADHD would gladly quit in a minute if they had the chance. One of their biggest problems is that children don't get to change jobs!

Children with ADHD have a difficult time being systematic, accurate, methodical, organized and thorough. Their inattention and impulsivity lead to errors in reading, writing, spelling, math and picking up the room. These errors often cause others to label them as careless or lazy.

These children tend to act without thinking first, which can cause social difficulties. They have difficulty sitting still, waiting, being quiet and staying with one thing. They are likely to have trouble with sports that require a lot of waiting (e.g. baseball).

Other Special Challenges

ADHD symptoms are not the same in any two children. A child with ADHD may be bouncy and cheerful or withdrawn and grumpy, quietly spacey or constantly dashing about. Some children with ADHD have other special challenges.

Learning disabilities are found in 25 to 40 percent of children with ADHD. These difficulties may require changes in communication and teaching techniques. In other cases, learning difficulties may make children appear to have ADHD even when they don't.

A child who has trouble making sense of what she or he hears is likely to "tune out" of a lecture and do more interesting things, such as pestering her or his neighbor. *Keeping A Head in School* by Dr. Melvin Levine (Educators Publishing Service, 1990) is an excellent resource for parents and teachers of children with learning difficulties.

Oppositional defiant disorder is present in some children with ADHD (perhaps one-third). These children seem to be chronically argumentative. They easily loose their tempers and tend to refuse to do what is asked. They seem purposely to annoy others and are also easily annoyed themselves. They tend to blame others for their own mistakes, speak rudely, and be in a bad mood much of the time.

Preserving the self-esteem of a child with both oppositional disorder and ADHD is no easy task. Your own self-esteem often feels attacked. All children with ADHD are "parent expensive" and "teacher expensive," but the child with oppositional disorder as well is far more expensive, not only to others but to himself or herself. Parents and teachers of oppositional children need to gather all the support and skills they can.

Conduct disorder is rare in younger children with ADHD, and it is unlikely to develop if a child with ADHD maintains a good sense of self-esteem. Conduct disorder involves actions such as substance abuse, stealing, running away overnight, lying, setting fires, school truancy, breaking and entering, physical cruelty to animals, deliberate destruction of others' property, initiating fighting or using a weapon in a fight. Low self-esteem and severely impaired parent-child relationships tend to mark the slippery slope toward conduct disorder behaviors.

Most children with ADHD do not develop conduct disorder. However, children with ADHD are more likely than others to develop conduct disorder, particularly if they are also oppositional.

Early and sustained interventions appropriate for children with ADHD include educational services, medical therapy if indicated, and behavioral and emotional support. Parents of children with oppositional disorder and ADHD need energetic support and training. The child with conduct disorder symptoms needs prompt mental health assistance for child and family and is beyond the scope of this book.

Variations of attention deficit disorder exist. Not every child with attentional difficulties has the same degree of difficulty with hyperactivity, impulsivity and inattention. Some children, particularly girls, seem to have the most difficulty with inattention. They have a hard time staying on task and noting the important details in school. They may seem "spacey," but they do not get into the behavioral and social difficulties caused by impulsivity and hyperactivity.

Such children may be said to have ADD, leaving out the hyperactivity. Often their diagnosis is delayed because their inattention is primarily a problem to themselves, not to others.

Other children have intense difficulty with impulsivity, so that although they can build with Legos for hours, they make lots of impulsive errors on schoolwork and in social situations. Some very energetic children do not have ADHD at all, but are just born to move.

What the Problems Look Like

Now let's look a little more closely at the steering and braking difficulties that occur with ADHD. Every few years, experts get together to decide what to call "it" (in the past it's been called minimal brain dysfunction, minimal brain damage, hyperkinesis, hyperactivity syndrome) and what is needed to diagnosis it.

In general, a diagnosis of ADHD requires that problems of attentional focus and impulse control be significantly greater than normal for the age and sex of the child, be present at least six months and be evident in a number of different settings. (See Appendix E.)

Steering Problems

The steering problems *(a directional difficulty/attention deficit disorder)* take the form of inattentiveness and restlessness. The children have trouble coming to attention, continuing to concentrate, and changing just when others want them to. They can't seem to get their attention to lock in to the right thing.

It's kind of like a radio that has a lousy "adjacent channel reject system," so that all the stations are coming in at once. These children's systems make it difficult to select just one input channel.

Children with ADHD are very distractible. Things in their environment and their own ideas seem to draw their attention like a magnet. They are distracted by sights, sounds and touch. They are distracted by other people, particularly other students. They seem compelled to intrude, interrupt and touch. They are distracted by the other side of the fence—the things they don't have, the places they are not, and the people they aren't with.

The child who has been begging for weeks to go on a special outing may begin to ask what you're going to do afterward within ten minutes of being there. The child who has just opened ten birthday presents gets upset that that's all. Whatever toy another child has is what he or she wants, while his or her own toys lie untouched.

For these children, their own ideas are magnetic, a particular challenge for the bright child with ADHD, who daydreams, blurts out answers, and starts talking about interesting things that have no apparent connection to what anyone else is thinking about. The urge to move and change is another magnetic attraction, easily observed in the child's fidgeting, frequent departures from the chair, and difficulty in staying with a single task.

Children with ADHD tend to make aiming errors, not focusing their attention in the right direction at the right time. Their attention wanders. They tend to notice and recall things that others (and even they themselves) don't consider very important, while missing the important stuff. These children want to pay attention to the important stuff, but the loose steering makes it hard to go in the right direction.

They miss the main point in instructions and information, in emotional expressions and social interactions. They are likely to be unaware that someone is joking or that someone is getting fed up. They also tend to be "leaky" with their belongings, losing and misplacing them with frustrating regularity, because they don't pay attention to what they are holding and don't notice when their hands open and they drop the object.

Braking Problems

Problems with speed control *(hyperspeed/hyperactivity)* involve poor regulation of action and mood.

Children with ADHD tend to go too fast or too slowly. How many times does the impulsive child hear, "If you'd only slow down..."? But their brakes just don't work well on those hills. These children tend to do things too fast, with results that look careless.

At other times they may get tired or have trouble getting started, so they do things too slowly. They may get stuck in one place, repeating the same thing, unwilling to change tasks, showing a tendency to perseverate, i.e., persist in inappropriate behavior.

Children with ADHD fire first and aim later. They are impulsive. They have trouble waiting their turn.

They tend to answer before they have read or heard (much less thought about) the question and to do assignments without reading instructions. They also have a tendency to dash and dart, sometimes endangering themselves. They may be destructive and later regret it.

Their impulsive lack of reflection leads to a tendency to be oblivious to the feelings, perspectives and needs of others. They seem to be difficult to influence with positive or negative consequences, reason, values or goals, because their systems do not allow them to pause long enough to check out the "Caution!" and "Do I want to do this?" files before the action is done.

It has been said of children with ADHD that you can't train them for love or money. That is an exaggeration, but there's enough reality in it to caution the critics and comfort the struggling parent and teacher. The younger and more impulsive the child, the truer it may be. One of the greatest potential benefits of medication is that it may allow a pause for reflection that allows the child to check and choose, to get ready and aim before she or he fires.

Children with ADHD have difficulty controlling their moods. They are emotionally labile, prone to get hysterically silly and giddy, and equally likely to dissolve in a flood of tears, or to explode in fury, all with little provocation. One note of caution: This emotional lability tends to get worse as medication is wearing off, a situation called *rebound*. If this is happening, check with the prescribing physician about modifying the dose to minimize such difficulties.

Making It Easier

A bike with poor steering and loose brakes would be easier to ride on a broad, uncrowded path than on a crowded, windy, narrow path. Similarly, children with ADHD do much better with fewer distractions and a clear view of the road in front of them.

They do better with regular schedules that let them know what's ahead. They do better when supportive adults help them keep steering on the right path. They do better on paths they know.

They have difficulty with new people, settings and experiences. They need good road signs—external organization, regulation and identified expectations. They need "rubber walls" that guarantee they stay on the right paths without getting hurt.

For all their differences, children with ADHD are primarily children. They need food, warmth, safety, love, fun and freedom. They need a sense of belonging and security, of competence and power. And they need freedom from embarrassment. They have unique individual strengths and struggles, and our greatest challenge is to nurture their gifts.

Chapter 2

Understanding What's Different: Diagnosing and Demystifying

One of the toughest things about dealing with the child with ADHD is that ADHD is an invisible handicap, and the behaviors that characterize it might be described as careless and irritating. However, research on ADHD clearly indicates that it has a physical cause. Like near-sightedness, the condition is much more difficult to deal with if you don't recognize it.

Diagnosing and demystifying, identifying and explaining the cause or causes of problems, are the first steps in helping the challenging and challenged child. Knowing that some bikes have loose steering and brakes doesn't necessarily mean that loose steering and brakes are causing *my* bicycle to go through stop signs. Maybe I'm not used to hand brakes. Maybe the gears are stuck, or I'm thinking about something else, or I can't see the signs because the sun is in my eyes.

Someone knowledgeable about bikes and cycling needs to do some looking and ask some questions before he or she can decide what changes are needed and what tools to use. He or she makes a *diagnosis*, then explains it to me *(demystifies it)*, and proceeds to help correct the difficulties with tools, training or both.

Diagnosing means determining if the child's symptoms (signs of problems) are caused by ADHD or contributed to by other diagnoses (causes of problems) he or she may have. The diagnosis enables us to treat not only the ADHD, if present, but other contributing problems as well.

What Else Could It Be?

The following diagram summarizes the differential diagnosis for ADHD—the various causes of inattention and restlessness. A child might have one or several of the diagnoses, with or without ADHD. I divide the different possible causes of the symptoms into primary, secondary and tertiary causes.

Primary causes refer to brain-based ADHD, the loose steering and brakes.

Causes of Attention Problems

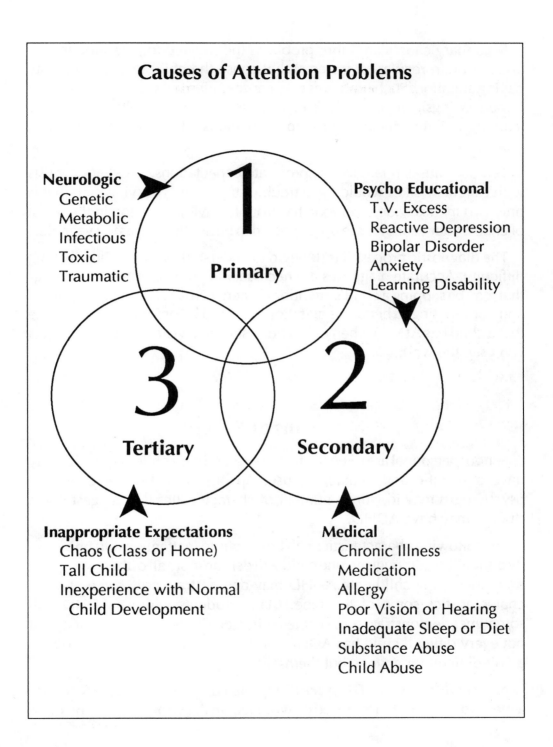

Neurologic
Genetic
Metabolic
Infectious
Toxic
Traumatic

Psycho Educational
T.V. Excess
Reactive Depression
Bipolar Disorder
Anxiety
Learning Disability

1 Primary

3 Tertiary

2 Secondary

Inappropriate Expectations
Chaos (Class or Home)
Tall Child
Inexperience with Normal
    Child Development

Medical
Chronic Illness
Medication
Allergy
Poor Vision or Hearing
Inadequate Sleep or Diet
Substance Abuse
Child Abuse

Secondary causes are other problems (not related to persisting imbalance of brain regulation systems) that cause the child to have difficulty paying attention. Such problems may cause restlessness, emotional lability (mood swings), impulsiveness or aggression. They involve the child's learning abilities, health and emotional status. (These are discussed in more detail in Appendix B.)

Tertiary causes relate to inappropriate expectations. Excellent cyclists with excellent bikes would have trouble staying on a curving path that is only two inches wide. Everyone has trouble paying attention in the midst of chaos. Four year olds are not expected to be as attentive as ten year olds.

The diagnostic process lets us begin to understand why a child is having difficulty. Accurate diagnoses are necessary to address the various things that may be sapping a child's attentional energy, frustrating her or his efforts and contributing to her or his agitation. It would be unfortunate to assume that a child has ADHD when in fact he or she has a vision problem and just can't see the work.

Symptoms at School

School personnel are often the first to suggest that a child's struggles may have a specific and treatable cause. An observant teacher or school psychologist may identify a number of characteristics that suggest that a student may have ADHD.

The following characteristics can be tip-offs to inattention and impulsivity difficulties, although no one child will demonstrate all of these struggles. Remember, any child with ADHD may demonstrate only some of these characteristics some of the time. Many students without ADHD will sometimes demonstrate some of these characteristics. Remember, too, that not every difficult child has ADHD, and that some children with ADHD aren't difficult for anyone but themselves.

Most children with ADHD are disorganized. A messy backpack echoes a messy desk. Papers are curiously wrinkled, in the wrong place, and often lost. A mysterious black hole seems to swallow papers, books, permission slips and assignment sheets as they travel to and from school.

The book for the assignment hides when it is needed, while other things in the desk distract the attention that was supposed to be used to find the book. Transitions from one topic to the next cause agitation and confusion. Sequences are difficult, and stories are told out of order.

Reading is typically impulsive. Children with ADHD don't stop to think about which side of the line has the hump, even though they can tell a *d* from a *b* if they stop to think about it. They read the first one or two letters of a word and guess the rest of the word.

They frequently substitute words (such as *a* for *the*). They tend to skip words and lines and lose their place, particularly while other students are reading.

Writing varies in quality due to impulsivity. Students with ADHD can write nicely on occasion, but usually they act rushed. They run words together. They write over, erase (often tearing through the paper) and make spelling errors frequently. They write with varying pressure.

Lack of planning results in starting in the middle and crowding at the end of a line. Letters keep changing form (the same letter may be drawn in four different ways on one page), slant in varying directions and don't stay on the line. Copying errors are frequent.

Math mistakes often relate to the inaccurate copying of numbers or signs and poor column arrangement. Children with ADHD often do the problem without noticing the sign of the problem (add, subtract, multiply). They misread (or fail to read) word problems and lesson instructions. They often solve problems in random order and skip problems.

Their drawings often show stick figures, faces only, or other rapidly done forms, although they may be magnificent in complexity. Coloring tends to be jerky, often outside of the line, and energetic. The quality of drawings may vary greatly.

Children with ADHD have trouble with the pace of the classroom. They raise their hands but don't know the answer when called on. (By then they have probably thought of five other things.) They talk out of turn, a reasonable though disruptive way of sharing information before it's forgotten.

Their minds travel far from the subject at hand while waiting for others to be called on. They are often unclear on the assignment given when they weren't paying attention, so they need to ask their neighbors. They move quickly from high energy to intense fatigue. They have trouble stopping behavior at the moment they are asked to do so.

Their restlessness leads to visits to the bathroom, the pencil sharpener and the wastebasket. They may seem to need to move from sitting to kneeling to standing (and sometimes climbing up on the desk) in order to concentrate. They have trouble waiting in line, because it's hard for them to stand still.

*They also have touching trouble*s. They're likely to fidget with the hair or clothing of a nearby classmate—whatever is handy—which may not be appreciated by the other child. On the other hand, if someone bumps into them, they may respond as though they've been intentionally struck, without reflecting on the accidental nature of the contact.

They often seem out of step with their classmates. Tendencies to moodiness and perseveration can cause them to embarrass themselves with outbursts atypical for their age.

Because they frequently feel out of control, they may spend playground time trying to boss peers or find a secure niche in a clearly defined pecking order by playing with children several years older or younger. In preschool and kindergarten, children don't pay much attention to what anyone else is saying, but by second grade, many peers may find these children offensive or weird because of their poor listening skills and tendency to make unrelated comments.

Children with attention deficit disorder who are *not* hyperactive may be quite lost in the classroom but difficult to identify. They tend to quietly float, never quite sure of the lesson or the assignment, out of step but not disruptive. Confusion, daydreaming and incomplete assignments in a "sweet" child who is performing below potential indicate the possibility of ADD.

Although children with ADHD demonstrate distress when they fail at tasks, they don't seem to do the things necessary to succeed, which can be particularly frustrating to parents and teachers. Remember the boy riding the bike at the park who couldn't get his bike to go where he wanted it to go, or stop when he wanted it to? He didn't intend to make his parents angry; he just couldn't control the bike.

The same is true for these frustrated children with ADHD. Nagging and lectures and punishments don't make the steering and brakes work. They just whittle away at these children's self-esteem.

Getting Help

The concerned classroom teacher can seek assistance from other staff members. Have they also been concerned about the child? If problems have not been encountered in other classrooms, consider investigating new stresses on the child and modifying classroom management as the first steps.

Is there any existing assessment data or medical history that will help you understand and assist the child? Have others found ways to help this student? Who will be part of the team to begin an assessment?

Because ADHD and learning disabilities often overlap, school psychoeducational assessment is usually appropriate. School assessment responsibilities for ADHD and testing indicators of ADHD are discussed in Appendix C.

Teachers need to share their concerns with the child's family and help the family get outside assistance. Although schools may provide psychoeducational assessment, they generally cannot provide the medical assessment that should be part of the evaluation of any struggling child. The physician should receive a clear description of the child's classroom struggles and copies of any prior assessments from school staff.

Teachers who recommend a medical assessment will find many parents grateful; but in some cases the family may be confused, reluctant, even defensive. Family members may feel that the school is trying to label the child to make up for the school's shortcomings. They may be afraid that something is really wrong. It may be beneficial to invite such parents to observe the class, because some students with ADHD cope reasonably well outside of the very distracting and demanding environment of school.

When school staff speak with families about medical assessment, they should avoid diagnosing ("Your child is ADHD or hyperactive") or prescribing ("He needs medicine"). Emphasize that the child is struggling and that something has been interfering with the success the child desires.

Explain the connection between diagnosis and appropriate assistance. You may want to share the diagram of the various causes of inattention and restlessness. You may also want to share the bicycle analogy. This analogy can be related to the following examples of common medical diagnoses with which families may be familiar, diagnoses that also have an impact on a child's school performance.

People who wear glasses had to get a diagnosis to find out why they had trouble seeing the blackboard or reading. The tool that fixes their vision is the pair of glasses they wear. They check back with the doctor from time to time to see if they need a different prescription.

They have to remember where they put their glasses when they take them off. When it rains, the glasses get wet and they can't see, so they have to wipe off the lenses as soon as they're inside. But otherwise, it's no big deal.

If a person is always tired and cold and has dry skin and dry hair, the body's thyroid gland may not be making enough thyroid hormone. When thyroid levels are low, the brain doesn't work well. A medical history and exam lead the doctor to order tests to make the diagnosis. A small tablet of thyroid medicine, taken daily, is the tool that renews warmth, energy, shiny hair and clear thinking.

An earache or plugged ears may interfere with school performance. The doctor looks in the ear to make the diagnosis. Then he or she decides if ear drops are needed to treat a problem outside the eardrum or if medicine should be taken by mouth to treat an infection on the inside. The child may need to sit near the teacher for better hearing until his or her ears are normal.

A diagnosis of ADHD would be another reason for a child to be seated fairly near the teacher, to decrease distraction. In order to make a diagnosis of ADHD, a doctor would ask questions, review parent and teacher rating scales and any other observation or assessment records, do an exam and observe the child in the office. The doctor would also be checking for any of the other things, like plugged ears, allergies or low thyroid, that might make it more difficult for a child to perform up to ability.

Sometimes teachers or families are reluctant to involve a physician because they're concerned that the doctor might prescribe medication. Medication for ADHD is like pliers for a bike with loose steering and brakes. The medication allows the child better control, but the child decides which paths to take.

Used every day, the medicine helps the body have a better balance of the regulating chemicals that allow the child to select, choose, stop, pay attention and concentrate more easily. With proper dosages, medicine does not decrease a child's energy for sports and other activities, but helps the child channel the energy more appropriately. (For more information about medication, see Chapter 3 and Appendix F.)

A Word to Families

If you suspect ADHD in your child, you should first contact your child's physician and your child's school. Ask your physician if she or he does special assessments for children having learning, behavioral or attentional problems (fifteen minutes is not enough!). If your physician doesn't do these assessments, the physician or the local Learning Disabilities Association can refer you to physicians who do.

At school, talk with the teacher about your concern and ask for help from the school student study team (child study team, student assessment team). If you need further assistance, tell the resource specialist, a teacher with extra training to help children with learning disabilities, that you would like an IEP (Individualized Educational Plan) for your child. The public school is required to provide testing within several months of a signed request.

How a Diagnosis Helps

A well-explained diagnosis of ADHD may bring profound relief to child, parent and teacher. It can be a first step in rebuilding the self-esteem of all involved.

The diagnosis sheds light on the mystery of the inconsistencies. The student's talents and interests, often hidden by the steering and speed control difficulties, need to be highlighted, for they are the tools for positive change.

Parents and teachers need to understand that the child does not intend to be difficult. At the same time, they are assured that the biologic problems are not caused by parenting or teaching history.

The child needs to be relieved of the sense of being stupid, crazy or bad. An analogy such as that of the boy whose bike has loose steering and brakes may help the child understand that she or he, like that boy, is being frustrated by a biological handicap. And even though it can cause complications in many areas, the problem is limited and can be dealt with.

Chapter 3

Tools of the Trade: Strategies for Coping with ADHD

Diagnosis and demystification are only first steps in regenerating self-esteem in a child with ADHD. Even if medication is used, many of the symptoms continue.

Let's go back and watch the family biking through the park—the one with a boy on a bike that has loose steering and brakes. Why are the parents yelling at the boy? They think he's goofing off. But what if they knew that the steering and brakes don't work well? Do you think they'd still yell?

Well, they might. They might yell to warn him of something in the path that he hasn't seen yet. They might yell because they're afraid he's going to hurt himself or someone else, or just to give him the extra time he needs to get around something.

The parents probably feel responsible for the boy. If they didn't know him or care about him, they might just ignore him. That would mean that he wouldn't be yelled at, but then he might crash more often.

On the other hand, the yelling can be a problem, too, even though it might be needed in an emergency. It might make the boy look at the parents instead of where he's going, which might make him more likely to crash. If the family is biking on a busy, winding pathway and the boy's bike has loose steering and brakes, no one is going to have a very good time.

The boy will probably feel frustrated by his bike, even though everyone admires how wonderful and fast it is. The parents and the boy may feel angry at each other and guilty that they feel angry and aren't having fun together. All those feelings probably spoil the fun for any brothers, sisters or friends who might be along, too.

How can this family have a good time biking together? Let's look at six tools that can assist them, tools that can be remembered as ABCDEF.

- *A* is for ***adaptations*** that can be made. The family can find paths that are broad and uncrowded, to avoid the need for sharp turns and sudden stops.

- *B* is for ***behavior management strategies*** that can be set up, such as warning signals the parents can use instead of yelling to let the boy know there is a turn or stop ahead.

- **C** is for ***cognitive-behavioral training***. The boy is assisted in thinking about solutions to challenges and using the strategies. For example, he can learn to use the gears to help him slow down and to look farther ahead to give himself time to steer around a pothole.

- **D** is for ***diagnosing, demystifying*** and ***doing*** something to tighten the brakes and steering. The family might use a wrench or pliers to fix the bike. If the brakes and steering tend to work loose when the boy's riding, it's probably a good idea for the family to bring the pliers along. In a child with ADHD, **D** also stands for ***drug therapy.***

- **E** is for ***esteem,*** for ***enjoy,*** for ***extra-curricular.*** **E** is also for ***esteem building,*** the ways of talking and treating each other that say each person is important. It stands for all the other things (such as having a snack, chasing butterflies, singing silly songs) that the family might enjoy when they're on a bike trip, things that remind them how much they like each other and themselves and being alive. Since the boy's bike is excellent at going up hills, the family might enjoy riding to the top of a hill with a beautiful view and walking back down.

- **F** is for ***feelings***—understanding where they come from and dealing with them, both good and bad. The parents may not realize how bad their yelling makes the boy feel. They may not be aware of the worry that's causing the yelling. Maybe someone else can help them see what's happening, so they can use the ABCD tools with more care, to protect self-esteem and feelings.

A—Adaptations

B—Behavior management strategies

C—Cognitive-behavioral training

D—Diagnose, demystify, drug therapy

E—Esteem

F—Feelings

You know, all the tools we've talked about would make for a more enjoyable bike trip for everyone, even without loose steering and brakes. Likewise, those same tools, except drug therapy, can be used whenever any child is having problems paying attention. They are especially important for the child with ADHD.

We'll discuss general principles of the first four tools (ABCD) in this chapter. Esteem and Feelings will have their own chapters. Then we'll go on to many specific examples which can help on the journey of all children through the classroom and home, particularly benefiting those with ADHD.

Adaptations

Adaptations can be made in environment, actions, schedules or expectations. Choose them based on what's very difficult and what's easy for the child. Adaptations are needed both for the realities of childhood itself and the special challenges of ADHD in particular. Adaptations help children win when they want to.

Most adaptations helpful to a child with ADHD are helpful to most children, whether in class or at home. Adaptations in environment, schedules and parenting and teaching styles can make the day go more smoothly for everyone.

Such adaptations can minimize distractions, provide a sense of predictability for children and help children make transitions. They should be designed to accommodate fluctuating energy levels and emphasize the most important things.

For the child with behavioral difficulties, adaptations would include close supervision to avoid guaranteed trouble situations for restless, impulsive children. Such situations include standing in line or sitting close to others at circle time or on the bench during baseball practice.

Behavior Management Strategies

Consequences of our behavior make it more or less likely that we will repeat that behavior. When teachers and parents use behavior management as a good tool, they select a behavior that they want to keep or get rid of and either reinforce it by repeating and rewarding it or try to extinguish it by ignoring or punishing it.

Behavior management happens whether we plan it or not. Every time I give in to a whining child I am "behaviorally reinforcing" the whining. The child is more likely to whine again.

Good behavior management is very important for children with ADHD, and the younger the child is, the more difficult and important good behavior management is. We use it to define and reinforce limits and rules to help guide children in spite of impulsivity. It also helps us give children the motivational energy necessary to focus their attention.

Remember that the brain of the child with ADHD lacks a good regulatory system. That regulatory system should be causing the child to wait to act ("fire") until there has been "ready, aim" time—time to check on goals and previous experiences of costs and rewards.

When the regulator isn't functioning properly, the child's impulsive action takes place before thinking, unless there's a very strong, fast, guiding message getting through to say "Stop!" Consequences, both positive and negative, are part of our efforts to build those guides.

The Underlying Concepts

Several important concepts underlie behavioral management.

Be consistent in not rewarding unwanted behavior. Inconsistent rewards encourage a behavior to be repeated, whether the behavior is desired or undesired.

Unfortunately, if I reward a child inconsistently for whining, sometimes holding firm and sometimes giving in, I have put her or him on a "variable reinforcement schedule." That occasional reward makes the behavior much harder to get rid of than if I rewarded the child all the time for whining, and then stopped completely.

Let's take the example of a candy machine. Each time you put the coin in and pull the handle, you get some candy. One day, you see someone get a candy bar by hitting the machine. You try it, and it works.

You try again several times but don't get another candy bar—until the fourth try. That will keep you going for quite a while longer, and if you succeed on the ninth and the fifteenth tries, you're likely to hit candy machines the rest of your life even if you never get another candy bar.

Now imagine that, after years of regularly receiving the candy you pay for, you get no candy for your money five times in a row. You begin to doubt that candy machines work any more (the way they used to).

If you pay ten times without getting the candy, your previous 55 successful experiences would not convince you to continue where the last ten had failed. Your candy-buying behavior would have been extinguished, and your machine-hitting behavior fairly well established.

Punishing doesn't work nearly as well as reinforcement and ignoring. Punishment tends to cause anger, which decreases the desire to do well. It is also a "soggy potato chip." When a child is hungry, a soggy potato chip is better than none. Children who crave our attention are happier if we yell at them than if we don't pay them any attention at all.

Use rewards (and logical consequences) to increase the attentional energy these children need to stay focused. I'm repeatedly impressed with the power of promised stickers (liberally dispensed on a frequent basis) to energize the attention-fatigued young ADHD student during testing. Good grades and good wages are motivating consequences for older folks. Unfortunately, children with ADHD may receive few rewards because the usual requirements to succeed are beyond their reach.

Use rewards to eliminate unwanted behavior. One good way to get rid of an unwanted behavior is to reward another behavior that can't happen at the same time. Let's say I want to get a child to stop hitting and kicking things and other people when angry. I can reward the child for clapping her hands or stomping his feet when angry, because you can't hit and kick while you're stomping and clapping. (Of course, I would need to clarify that I wouldn't give the reward if the child was hitting or kicking just before or after the stomping and clapping.)

Response cost systems are generally necessary for the child with significant ADHD symptoms. A response cost involves an immediate and non-emotional small loss as soon as an unwanted behavior occurs. The response cost should be matter-of-fact and predictable; it is meant to teach and define, not hurt. For example, give a child credit for 25 pennies a day. Each time the child is rude, say, "That's rude (or "That hurts"). You lose a penny."

Be prepared for resistance. "I don't care" is a predictable and irrelevant defense of a child in the face of behavioral guidelines and consequences. The child makes the statement in an attempt to suggest that the system has no power, but such a statement does not change the power of good behavior management plans. The only adult response needed is, "Nevertheless...."

Systems That Work

There are lots of behavior management systems, and lots of good books with excellent ideas for home and classroom. As you come up with your own systems, keep the following points in mind:

- Target behaviors should be carefully chosen to reflect what's really important. They should be clearly stated and limited in number.

- Reward whenever possible, but only reward behaviors you want to continue. Always try to think of the positive behavior you can reward instead of the negative behavior you want to punish.

- Ignoring works better than punishing to get rid of unwanted behavior. Behavior that is never rewarded in any way tends to stop, but behavior that is rewarded some of the time is the hardest to get rid of.

- Consequences should be immediate (within the child's time view). They should be based on things important to the child (but please don't take away activities in his or her main area of interest and skill). They should also be based on fact and known rules, not emotion.

- Use logical consequences whenever possible. For example: Papers turned in on time get a bonus. Toys left out get put into a bag for a week.

- Consequences should involve the least reward or cost that will modify behavior. Don't choose a cost that you're reluctant to use. You're likely to fudge on imposing the consequence, and be more penalized than the child if you do use it.

- Consequences should also be available for use during the whole day. If the first mistake uses up the only consequence (e.g., a note home), what do you do for the rest of the day?

- Specific systems for behavior management need novelty, variety and brevity. Change the game often.

Behavior management strategies work best when founded on a positive, caring relationship. They need to be non-embarrassing and fair. They should focus on a single behavioral issue at a time. Don't, for instance, mix "no talking out of turn" with "no hitting."

To improve self-esteem, try to make it very likely that the child will succeed. Graduate the requirements from a sticker for each ten minutes of silence to increments of twenty to thirty minutes of silence, then to an hour or half a day of silence. The child who wins at the beginning will keep playing the game.

Let children work their way out of the doghouse if you put them in. Letting children work out of trouble:

- lets by-gones be by-gones

- helps keep your consequences available all day—after all, if a child is in the doghouse already, where can you put him or her for the next goof?

ᴥ lets children regain self-esteem—and that's what this book is about.

When rewarding a group or the whole class, do not single out a particular child who is "losing" the reward for the group. You may single out the child whose good behavior is the basis for rewarding the group. ("Thanks for sharing your eraser, Sean. Point.")

The two most difficult problems for behavior management involving several or many children are (1) adjusting fairly to individual differences (like ADHD) and (2) protection from embarrassment. With children of different abilities and challenges, behavioral systems need to be individualized.

Behavior management strategies that are embarrassing are punishment; they are soggy potato chips that rob self-esteem. You may have seen a child become the "class clown," apparently trying to get his or her name on the board one more time. Such clowning can be a survival skill for an impulsive child whose biologic system makes it very difficult to keep quiet anyway. Don't embarrass this child.

Bonus Points: A Strategy in Action

How can you individualize and not embarrass students in a class of 33? One teacher copied "bonus" pages. On each page, the names of all the students in her class were listed down the left side, with twenty-four columns across the page. At the top of each column was room to write (sideways) things for which the students could earn bonus points, such as "papers in on time" or "golden silence" while working on a particular assignment.

The teacher would announce a different bonus challenge to fit the needs of the day and write it on the board just before the challenge began. Each day a fresh page went on her clipboard, to be filled with up to 24 bonus challenges, four per hour.

Whenever she came to a bonus request time (papers in, golden silence), she wrote it at the top. When the time was up, she'd draw a line down the column, interrupting the line where she knew someone had not been successful or was absent.

She took five to ten private minutes at the end of the day to tally up the "line-throughs" for each student. According to a prior formula, a child who

Bonus Points Sample Chart

Names	Quiet entry	Math worksheet	Clean desk	Book ready	Golden Silence #1	Cooperating quietly	Spelling assignment	Singing along	Golden Silence #2
Beatrice	│	│	│			│			│
Ben		│						│	│
Edie	│								
James			│						│
Hector	│		│		│				│
Kendra					│	│			
Michelle		│				│			
Mieko		│		│			│	│	
Nate		│		│		│	│	│	

had a great deal of difficulty being quiet or organized might get the same credit for half the number of line-throughs as a mellow child for whom being quiet and organized was biologically easy.

At the beginning of the school year, the teacher tallied the line-throughs in the middle of the day, giving the students a noon report as well as a report the following morning. Several children continued to receive private noon reports throughout the year.

The teacher used the pages all year, but she would use the bonus points for different kinds of rewards. Each Monday she'd announce what the week's bonus rewards would be. The students were encouraged to keep their earnings private.

Time Out

A word about "time out" is in order. Time out is, by definition, embarrassing in a classroom. However, it is the logical consequence of any aggressive behavior with which children have already embarrassed themselves.

When time out is used as a consequence of antisocial behavior, the child should be out of contact with anyone else. Time spent sitting distracting the nurse or guidance counselor or screaming at mother from across the room is not time out.

Children should be in time out for as many minutes as they are years old. (We'll talk about "reset time," which is different and important when a child is out of control, in Chapter 5.) *The Time Out Solution* by Lynn Clark (Contemporary Books, 1989) is an excellent resource for time-out strategy.

Cognitive-Behavioral Training

Cognitive-behavioral training involves teaching the child cognitive or thinking methods and rewarding the child's efforts to use those methods.

Such methods are most effective in the framework of the child's values and goals, likes and dislikes. Children with ADHD benefit especially from cognitive-behavioral training in impulse control ("stop-think" training), organization, relaxation and social skills.

The following conditions must be met for effective cognitive-behavioral training.

- The child needs to identify that she or he has an area of difficulty and to want to gain skills to deal with it.

- Training must be spread over time and circumstance with reinforcement to permit generalization and continued use.

- Training should begin with small, concrete tasks before moving to more abstract, general tasks.

- The use of the strategies or steps, not the final outcome, should be rewarded.

Teachers can adapt available curricula to an entire class, or training can be done by counselors or therapists with small groups. Both parents and teachers should understand and model, incorporate and reinforce what the child is learning.

Stop-Think

Children can be helped to accept their impulsivity (speed spurts) and identify circumstances in which the impulsiveness interferes with their goals or the well-being of others. They are taught techniques to stop themselves before acting to ask: What's going on here? What am I being asked to do? What's the problem? Then they reflect on various possible courses of action.

The final step is self-assessment and encouragement, either "Whoops, not quite right, but I'll do better next time" or "Yes! Good job!" More information can be found in the *Stop and Think Workbook* by Phillip Kendall (see Suggested Readings).

Academic Organization

Most children with learning or attention difficulties need assistance with study skills. Study skills curricula can be incorporated into daily classwork or offered in summer school. The entire class can benefit because such a curriculum improves the chance that each student will apply the skills to a variety of appropriate academic tasks.

Entire elementary schools have adopted Anita Archer and Mary Gleason's excellent study organization skills curriculum, *Skills for School Success* (Curriculum Associates, 1989), either during the school year or during the summer.

Relaxation and Calming Strategies

Children with ADHD tend to have "stuck mood control knobs." They may be able to avoid some of that emotional intensity and its consequences by learning self-relaxation strategies. Parents and teachers can help by giving such children cues or reminders to relax before they lose control.

Relaxation strategies are helpful skills for everyone. Visual imagery, aikido, meditation, biofeedback, deep breathing and stretching exercises are effective relaxation methods.

You can use visual imagery relaxation with a group of students. Have the students close their eyes. Narrate a soothing scene, being sure to stay away from content areas that might provoke anxiety in the students. (Floating on a cloud or floating down on a parachute, feeling warm breezes and looking down on pastoral scenery are great, unless you're afraid of heights.) Bedtime is a good time for parents to practice this technique, perhaps rubbing the child's back while the child rests in bed, eyes closed.

Gradually, you can begin to have children do their own narrating out loud in response to a single word *(cloud, parachute).* They might take turns, eyes closed, telling something they see.

The final step is for children to become able to envision and think of the relaxing scenario themselves, so that just the reminder of the word can enable them to initiate the calming visual imagery. *Smiling at Yourself* by Allen Mendler (ETR Associates, 1990) has other excellent relaxation imagery strategies.

Train students to use simple stretching, jogging in place and deep breathing exercises. Let them practice these techniques during homework breaks at home and during transitions in the classroom.

Safe ways to vent anger include writing down the angry feelings, fierce scribbling with a crayon (restricted to the paper), tearing a piece of paper into tiny pieces (over a wastebasket—or with the understanding that the child has to pick it up), pounding clay, hitting a tennis ball suspended in a small cloth bag, or punching a punching bag. (These techniques are discussed in more detail in Chapter 5.)

Remember, reward children for trying to use one of these strategies, even if they end up losing control. If trying is a success in itself, the child will try harder next time.

Social Skills Training

People have to pay attention to social cues not only for the sake of politeness but to understand what other people are saying and feeling. Activities that facilitate these skills include games in which children take turns acting out an emotion and guessing what is being acted, describing an experience and responding with a "how that must have felt" comment, guessing what characters in situation dramas might be feeling, or simply keeping track of how long they can maintain eye contact while communicating. These activities also help affective matching, an important skill in peer acceptance. (See the section on Fitting In in Chapter 4.)

Teasing is a big problem for children, particularly for those who overreact. One group of students learning to handle teasing developed and practiced a skit and made a videotape on ways of coping with teasing. They brainstormed good responses and then took turns acting out their suggestions.

One student would play the part of the teaser, and another the part of the student being teased. Even in that protected practice setting, the sting of teasing was felt and reacted to. But the students had professional guidance to "stop the action" and try again until they could really handle the situation.

One simple and effective response to teasing is, "Thanks for noticing." Reward the child for saying it. Also, as parent or teacher, model it in moments of a child's impulsive criticism. (Child: Your shirt's ugly. This test's too hard. Adult response: Thanks for noticing.) The barb is taken out of the attack, and with it the emotional escalation. In child-parent or peer-teasing interactions, the "thanker" always wins.

Listening to a tape of a group's conversation may help divergent ADHD children learn to listen for off-topic communication. They learn first to hear it in what is spoken and then in what they are about to say.

Lack of persistence at a task causes frustrating interruptions in activities. Provide external rewards for spending time on a given play activity. Children may also be taught to set goals and reward themselves both for sharing activities with a friend and for staying with an activity for a designated amount of time.

Children, particularly those with ADHD, often have difficulty dealing with failure. Helping someone else deal with failure can help children learn to cope with loss or failure themselves. A parent, teacher or therapist can model the frustration of losing in a board game as his or her piece is sent back several spaces: I'm not sure I want to play, I'm so far behind. Boy, I really don't feel good when I lose.

Children will tend to come to the aid of the distressed adult who is using I-statements. Such behavior is the first step in being able to aid themselves. From helping another through losses (while their own egos are safe), children begin to learn how to help themselves through losses.

The *Skill Streaming* series by Ellen McGinnis and Arnold Goldstein (Research Press, 1984) and the *Think Aloud* series by Mary Ann Bash and Bonnie Camp (Research Press, 1985) are excellent resources for social skills training. They can be used by school counselors or classroom teachers.

Drug Therapy

Medicine for ADHD is prescribed for the benefit of the child, not the parents or teachers. If the other tools (ABCEF) allow the child to succeed without medication, none is needed. Medication is indicated if the child with a diagnosis of ADHD is repeatedly unable to succeed at home, with friends or in school.

Lack of success is a serious threat to self-esteem. It can lead to depression and anxiety, as well as delay in skill development.

Medication should be tried before the child is so accustomed to failure that he or she has given up. It can be continued as many years as necessary (which may be through adolescence). While medication can be extremely helpful and is generally safe, careful management is required and side effects may be problematic, as discussed in Appendix F.

The Value of Pliers

Medicine is like the pliers used to tighten loose steering and brakes on the boy's bike. Even if a bike's steering is fixed, you can still crash it or run it off the road. The pliers don't drive the bike, and they don't make you a good cyclist. They just make it easier to steer the bike where you want it to go and stop it when you want to.

Likewise, medication for ADHD doesn't make anyone concentrate or be good or be smart. It just makes it easier for people to select what they want to do, think about or not do. It helps them stop long enough to think before acting. Children with ADHD who take medicine for it can talk out of turn, disrupt the class and make a mess at the table if they choose to, but it will be much easier for them to succeed when they try not to do those things.

Effective doses make it easier for children with ADHD to keep paying attention to what they choose, with less fatigue and increased alertness. Medication can help children slow down and think before acting, enabling them to learn strategies of long-term value.

Increased success improves self-esteem, as well as interactions with parents and teachers. Stimulant medication may decrease verbal and physical aggression.

Medication can help academic performance by improving writing, increasing time on task, and decreasing errors due to inattention and impulsivity. The ability to learn new things improves on low doses, although new learning is the first area of functioning to deteriorate when higher doses of medication are used.

Why Isn't Medicine Alone Enough?

First, medication doesn't work all the time. The more commonly used medicines have an effect similar to coffee; they decrease appetite and keep a person awake. Therefore, they are used only during the day, so the child can enjoy breakfast and dinner and still get adequate sleep. This means that the steering and brakes are loose much of the time that the child is home, even when medication is prescribed.

Second, if enough medication is used to fully control the restlessness and impulsivity, side effects, including headaches and irritability, are more common. The children begin to look like zombies, and the creativity needed for new learning is compromised (Douglas et al., 1988).

Tolerance (when the body gets rid of the medication too fast for it to work) develops more rapidly on high medication doses. Thus, the child treated with a dosage low enough to avoid side effects and tolerance may continue to be talkative and out of her or his seat a lot.

Finally, children with ADHD have not had experience planning and choosing effectively. In our bike analogy, if all the bikes the boy had ever ridden had loose steering and brakes, he would need to learn how to steer and brake once his new bike was working properly.

Medication gives children with ADHD new opportunities to stop and think, to reflect on promised rewards, goals, prior consequences and the feelings of self and others. But they need the benefit of the other ABCEF tools to learn how to make good choices.

Medication offers the greatest benefit when it's combined with appropriate educational and mental health assistance, as well as appropriate treatment of other causes of inattention and agitation.

Managing Medication

Ritalin and Dexedrine are the brand names for stimulants commonly used to treat ADHD. These drugs, like all medications, should be kept away from children. They should be kept in a locked place at school and in "parent-only" territory at home.

It is always an adult's responsibility to remind the child about taking any medication and to supervise the process. Children shouldn't have to experience an embarrassing loss of control because of delayed medication.

Children with ADD without hyperactivity also shouldn't miss medication. They may be very quiet and bother no one, but lose out on the afternoon's education.

Ritalin tablets are effective for only four hours in most students, and Dexedrine tablets for around five hours. Once the medication wears off, the child's steering and brakes are again out of whack, and it requires approximately thirty minutes for the next dose to take effect.

Children with ADHD are not likely to remember when they need their next medication dose, so adults must work out systems to ensure that students get their midday medication in time. Some teachers use a watch alarm (theirs or the student's) or a clock-radio alarm set to the appropriate time as a reminder of the medication time.

Communicate with the student's physician to time the medication to coincide with a natural transition time, such as when students are on their way to the playground or to lunch. The morning dose can often be moved around a bit to accommodate the school schedule. If the students go to lunch at 11:45, for instance, the morning dose of Ritalin would be given four hours earlier, at 7:45, unless school starts earlier than 8:15.

The medication tends to decrease appetite, so be sure the child eats a breakfast that contains some protein at the same time or before the medication is taken. If children are in school-based extended care, they may require an afternoon dose as well, three to four hours after the noon dose.

One school nurse made brightly colored plastic reminder cards for each student receiving any kind of medication. The cards are put in the boxes of the students' teachers at the end of each day. Teachers put the cards on their daily clipboards and hand them to students directly or under cover of a log sheet at medication time. Students turn the cards in to the nurse or health aide as they receive the medication.

The health office can then check on any students whose cards are not returned, and the returned cards are ready to put in teachers' boxes for the next day. All students receiving medication (antibiotics, cold and asthma medicines, etc.) use the same system, so students are less likely to attach any stigma to receiving the card reminder. Sensitive students may be given official responsibility for taking a daily log sheet to the office as a cover.

Some children may need to avoid a school medication dose because of teasing from peers or school difficulties in guaranteeing midday doses. Such children and their families should discuss with the physician the possibility of a long-acting form of the medication. Long-acting medication may also be more practical for children at camp.

Parent and teacher observations can help the physician maintain optimal medication dosages. Some children metabolize medication rapidly, so it is important to note the time of any recurring behavioral or academic problems.

Problems that consistently occur three and a half to four and a half hours after the morning dose may vanish if the second dose of medication is given at three hours for a child who metabolizes the medication rapidly. Parents and physicians may be grateful for a daily behavior log, which serves as an ongoing record of successes and difficulties as well as an excellent parent-teacher communication system. (It can also be used for a reward system.) A physician or school nurse may provide a checklist for ongoing monitoring.

Feeling OK About Taking Medicine for ADHD

How do children feel about taking medication for ADHD? In interviews, adults with ADHD recall having been embarrassed, particularly if comments were made in front of the class. They felt different from others, sensing that the medication signified that there was "something weird" wrong with them. Some just resented having to take the medicine without being able to explain why (Weiss and Hechtman, 1987, p. 296-300).

In considering the relationship between medication and the self-esteem of the child, embarrassment is clearly an issue. Parents and teachers should make every effort to protect the child's privacy. Long-acting medication, which avoids the need for a school dose, may be preferred for older, more-sensitive children to protect them from the perceived risk of "school exposure."

Give children ideas for discussing medication with their siblings and peers. One boy told curious peers that the medication was to treat his "allergy to noise." Many children feel comfortable just saying, "It helps me concentrate."

One little girl who is a leader in bringing ADHD "out of the closet" reported, "Johnny, Ben and Trevor use 'add' medicine too. Ben and I get to go get ours together." (*ADD* was pronounced as the opposite of subtract.) Others refer to the medicine, at least with their parents, as their "pliers."

The self-control issue is critical for the self-esteem of children taking medication for ADHD. Two things can be helpful.

First, help children understand that the medication is not there to control them, but to help them be in control. In the analogy of bicycles and pliers, ask children what happens to the bike and rider once the pliers have tightened up the steering and brakes. Clearly the riding is smooth, no more crashes.

Then ask if the pliers or the rider steered the bike away from the wall or thorny hedge. Children quickly realize that it was the rider—"Pliers can't steer!"

Medication can't make a person be good or bad. Medication just lets

I Can't Sit Still

children control which way they go because it lets their "chooser" (for concentration and actions) work.

Second, ask the physician to speak with the child regarding his or her feelings about the medication and to involve the child in choices about it. Possible child choices include:

- ❧ the exact time when medication is taken to fit the school lunch schedule
- ❧ how to make sure Mom or Dad can remember to give the medication at the right time
- ❧ deciding between a short- or long-acting medication

Children should have a chance to say how the medicine makes them feel. Do they feel better or worse? Do they feel it is a pretty good set of "pliers" or not so good?

At age nine or ten, children often decide to quit taking medication. Discuss this decision with the physician before the physician sees the child. Physician and child can discuss the child's sense that he or she can "handle it" without medication.

Physicians may give these children an opportunity to pursue this "experiment" for a period of one to four weeks. They can help children define clear parameters that would indicate that the pliers are still needed. When children feel empowered to participate in such a trial of being off medication, they are generally more able to acknowledge the ongoing need for those pliers if they have difficulties.

Prior development of cognitive strategies may improve a child's success while off medication. Teachers and parents should respect and assist children during these important trials. Respect for these ventures in autonomy is an important part of enhancing the child's self-esteem.

Chapter 4

The Self-Esteem Connection

Generally, children with ADHD have a very difficult time with self-esteem. Struggling with an invisible and inconsistent handicap they don't understand, they often experience rejection and failure, which may then be compounded by their own and others' negative expectations of them. The association of ADHD with learning disabilities or oppositional disorder can complicate the struggle for self-esteem.

Socially, children with ADHD may seek emotional intensity, both positive and negative. They tend to talk about things unrelated to the conversation or perspective of others and to be unaware of social clues. They also perseverate, repeating the same annoying words, questions or behaviors despite messages to stop.

In their desperate struggle to gain control, they are often bossy with peers and siblings. As a result of their multiple little aiming and speed errors, families and teachers may be chronically irritated by the interruptions, lost items, fidgeting, moodiness and strings of barely started projects.

Children with ADHD usually have numerous experiences of failure, especially in school, where failures include:

- poor grades

- visibly poorer output (cross-outs and wrinkled papers)

- rejection of their assignments

- high discipline rate, including class exclusion

- chronic peer exposure and humiliation

Used to rejection, these children expect to be rejected. Used to failure, they expect to fail. Others, too, may anticipate that children with ADHD will cause problems and overlook their talents and strengths.

Children with ADHD as well as their parents and teachers may be eagerly awaiting someone to help them understand, to act, to believe in themselves. The most important words come from the long term adult follow-up study by Weiss and Hechtman (1987): "When the adults who had been hyperactive were asked what had helped them most to overcome their childhood difficulties, their most common reply was that someone (usually a parent or teacher) had believed in them...."

Let's consider four major ingredients of self-esteem, as illustrated by the diagram of Esteem Kid. In our hearts, we need to feel *valued*. In our minds, we need to feel *in control*. In our muscles and other ways, we need to feel *capable*. And in the same way we need clothing, we need *protection from embarrassment*.

Esteem Kid

Feeling Valued

We all need to feel needed, enjoyed and wanted. We need to feel understood, at least part of the time. We want to have our ideas, feelings, frustrations and dreams respected. We want to be trusted. We need to be accepted with our differences.

Listening

To value a child, we must stop to listen. Spend time alone with the child to let this happen. For a teacher, this may mean asking the child with ADHD to spend five minutes as special assistant cleaning up the room at recess—a job of honor, not punishment. Then you can listen as the child rattles on—but really listen, don't just absent-mindedly nod your head.

If the excited child is telling a story in class at an inappropriate time, say, "Something is interesting. Tell me one word to remember it by, and then you can tell me about it later." Be sure to write down the word, so the child can tell you (or a friend) at an appropriate time.

This suggestion can be shortened to "One word?" and all the "one words" for each talkative student can be listed for later use. This technique not only brings the children back to attention in a positive way, it helps them practice pulling their thoughts into focus.

You may need to start by rewarding the child each time he or she can give you a one- or two-word summary. You can add a bigger reward as the number of times you ask for one word decreases because the child has learned to write down his or her own one word without talking at the wrong time. You are saying, "I value what you have to say, but I am teaching you how you can remember what you have to say until a good time to say it."

A similar system may help when a child is interrupting when a parent is on the phone or talking with someone else. But when it's not necessary to postpone the listening, listen attentively and immediately. It really is hard to put brakes on those ideas.

Sharing and Caring

Whenever possible, *say yes when invited*. As adults, we routinely impose our schedules on the child. The child asks us to play with trucks or dolls, and we say "later." Then we ask the child to enjoy a good time we have planned and are disappointed that our time is wrong for the child. Five minutes away from washing dishes to play trucks is worth fifty-five minutes in a counselor's office or at the zoo, if they are the child's five minutes.

Some school staff have developed a program to *"adopt" needy students*. The student meets with the adopting staff person (a secretary, an administrator, a teacher, but usually not the student's own classroom teacher) at least weekly.

Student and staff person may play a game of cards, play catch, share jokes and riddles, draw each other's portraits or read an exciting book. They celebrate birthdays and other special days. The adopting person may slip encouraging notes into the locker of the adoptee. The student is offered a listening ear when needed.

Honor the anger and tears, and laugh at the jokes. The anger will stop faster if you say, "That makes you so angry!" than if you say, "Stop being so angry." Anger is like pain. How do you stop hurting just because you are ordered to?

If jokes are the order of the day, enjoy the sublime to the ridiculous. At school, schedule a joke time for the joke experts of the room. Some of the jokes might be listed on the day's one-word list.

Call a bummer a bummer, but fondly. If something is tough, it's insulting to be told it's easy. If you know you've blown it, it's no help to be told everything is fine. How can children learn to accept and admit their mistakes if the mistakes are too terrible for you to mention? "That one got away" or "Whoops!" or "Bummer!" with an encouraging voice is a good response to the wrong answer.

Remember, children with ADHD will be excellent some of the time. Let them know you know that by acknowledging times when they miss the mark. Keep them headed for excellence, rather than hooked on mistakes. After all, erasers are made because people do make mistakes.

Expectations and Rewards

Expect excellence and lay out bridges to get the child there. Clearly state the expectation. For example: "The paragraph needs five sentences. The first one should introduce the subject. The words need to be written neatly and spelled correctly."

Then provide the who, what, when, where and how to enable it to happen: "First, write the main topic in the middle of the page. Good. Now write around it four or five things you want to say about it. Great." (or "Whoops! Those two need some more for company. Go round up two or three more ideas.") "Now number those things, so you know in what order you'll talk about them. That's your outline! Now write (or "tell me," if the child has trouble writing) a sentence for each one. Here you are. Now copy it very neatly. Excellent!"

Make corrections respectfully. Think of the highway patrol officer stopping the speeder. "Were you aware that you were going 70 in a 45-mile-per-hour zone?" the officer asks. Out comes the citation. All very courteous. No harangue, no anger.

The rule is clear, the observation defined. Just state the facts. There can even be a bit of respectful sympathy: "I guess your mind was somewhere else." No apologies, no changing the rule, just polite enforcement.

Of course, it's very important that the consequences be fair and do not insult the driver or make the officer reluctant to write the ticket when appropriate. The officer ordered to write a jail term for every speeder would be easily talked out of many of those tickets.

Similarly, the teacher who threatens to cancel a planned class outing if a child talks out of turn one more time may be easily deterred by pleas and promises. A private system involving immediate gain or loss of bonus points, symbolized by raffle tickets, plastic chips, cards or marks on a bonus page as described earlier, may serve as an effective classroom "ticketing" system.

A portable system for home use is tongue depressors. They are moved from the "excellent" to the "whoops" pocket if infractions occur. They may be moved back to the excellent pocket for some special good deed.

Keeping most of the sticks in the excellent pocket earns a tangible reward at the end of the day or outing. Ending up with all the sticks in the whoops pocket results in loss of a privilege.

This portable system can be used on outings for several children if each child has a different color of sticks. Children begin to focus much more energy on self-control as they see the sticks moving toward the whoops pocket.

Examine your own perceptions, expectations and feelings. I've become very fond of the bounce and sparkle, the creativity and unpredictability, the complexity and striving of my friends with ADHD, but it's easy to resent the need to be constantly on the alert.

Take some time to list what's good about your special child at school or home. If you can't find anything good, find someone to help you, and spend some time alone with the child until you can.

Feeling in Control

Feeling in control is no easy task when your steering and brakes are loose, whether you do or don't understand the problem. How do you say "You couldn't help it" and "Don't let it happen again" in the same moment?

We need to help children with ADHD understand that they are in the driver's seat, even if the steering is difficult. When discussing the loose steering and brakes analogy with children with ADHD, emphasize that the problem is lousy brakes and steering, not a lousy bike or driver.

Remind the child on medication that pliers make it easier to stop and steer the bike, but they don't do the stopping and steering. Only the rider can choose how and when and where to steer and brake. The pliers, the medicine, makes it easier for children to make their choices happen.

Can they crash the bike even when it's fixed? Sure. Can they "mess up" on medicine? Sure. But it's easier to avoid a crash. It's easier to keep concentrating and to think before they act.

Ask these children what they would do if they knew that the steering and brakes of their bike were loose and they were headed toward a big hedge with stickers. Some say, "Jump off." Others say, "Crash."

One said, "I'd start leaning long before I got there, so the bike would turn anyway." Another said, "I'd keep the seat low, so I could always put my feet down to stop first."

These last two children are realizing that they can be in control. Difficult to control doesn't mean out of control. This realization is the foundation for learning strategies for self-control. This is the first step in the cognitive-behavioral training discussed in Chapter 3.

All children benefit from strategies for organization, relaxation, social skills and impulse control, but children with ADHD are desperate for these coping techniques.

Teachers can use cognitive-behavioral systems to teach students better self-control in doing assignments. The child is trained step by step and rewarded for using the steps along the way.

A very simple example of cognitive-behavioral training in math is sign circling. Reward students with bonus points for circling the sign of each math problem before starting to solve it. Students learn a valuable strategy, checking to see if the sign is +, -, or x, to increase their chances of success.

In addition to strategies, **help children evolve values and goals.** The greatest feeling of being in control comes when we have been able to choose a goal as well as obtain it. Help children choose discrete achievable goals and the steps to work toward them.

In the largest and deepest sense, our beliefs determine the direction we will choose to aim our lives. The opportunity to develop our own faith, nurtured by the examples of others, anchors our sense of control.

Feeling Capable

Feeling capable evolves from knowledge, mastery, successful accomplishments and helping others. Experiences of independence, interdependence and overcoming are pivotal to an evolving sense of ability.

Knowledge and mastery are important. Children with ADHD may focus their knowledge on dinosaurs, baseball players or computers. They may master fishing, tennis, biking, photography, music, art or drama, as well as academics.

These children will be most able to know, master and accomplish in areas that fascinate them. Sustaining attention and effort for anything else may be too difficult. Use their interests. For example, if a child is avid about baseball, let him or her draw a map of the United States showing the home cities of all the major leagues.

Treat those areas to which the child is drawn very respectfully. Because it may seem that there is little that motivates children with ADHD, it is tempting to use an area they do enjoy as a "carrot" or "stick"—a privilege to be earned or lost.

On the school front, the most common example is prohibiting students who have academic difficulties from participation in sports, drama or other extracurricular activities. Those of us who care for children's self-esteem should advocate to preserve the children's right to do what they do well and what they enjoy. Don't take away the one activity that is enjoyable, successful and an area of potential mastery as a consequence for difficulties in other areas.

Helping is excellent therapy for everyone. Children with ADHD may be good at reading to younger children or good company for a pet. They may be able to run errands.

One of my friends with ADHD reported a single good day in his entire fourth-grade year. This was the day he got to be the voice of "Do-So," the puppet that went to kindergarten to talk about safety. This student is an entertaining conversationalist and competent reader, and he could have been used much more often.

Accomplishments may involve the successful completion of a contract, a job well done, chores, competitions or even high video game scores. Help children define tasks that can be completed, jobs that can be successfully done.

Start with a good brainstorm before a good outline. Start with a contract that rewards each half-hour a student doesn't call out in class before she or he tries to go for a whole day.

Guide children toward independence gradually. A study of 14-year-old boys indicated that the greatest correlate of delinquent behavior was early permission for autonomy. Those left to their own guidance while parents were at work were more likely to get into trouble than those in well-supervised programs.

Independence starts when a parent lets a little one walk next door alone while he or she watches. This independence slowly grows: up the block, across the street, to the park, to the store, riding a bike, taking the bus, then driving and going off to college.

Interdependent experiences, such as participation on a team or in a band or activities with friends and family, complement experiences of independence.

Successful interdependence and successful independence require adult guidance and selection blended with timely letting go. Children need adult guidance for a very long time, and children with ADHD are a bit more in need of that guidance. One of the dangers for these children is that they tend to wear out adults, who let go in exhaustion before it is time.

Protection from Embarrassment

Protection from embarrassment is remarkably difficult to manage in school, but it is extremely important. It's not easy at home, in sports, or in front of friends and acquaintances either. Impulsivity and inattention tend to put children with ADHD in embarrassing situations without any help from adults, but we often make it much worse.

Goof Insurance

Children with ADHD need "goof insurance," help in avoiding difficult situations. Some children with ADHD have consistent difficulty on the playground, where there aren't enough adults to guide them and their peers away from confrontation and eruption.

Goof insurance for such a child might include providing a coached game on the playground or having the child help set up the cafeteria instead of going outside. As cafeteria worker, the child could have the privilege of selecting one classmate to work with him or her each day.

In the classroom, the ADHD child is particularly likely to goof at staying still. Asking this child to run an "errand" may provide goof insurance and allow you to avoid penalizing her or him for out-of-seat behavior. If such students tend to get distracted and off-course, wandering about the school as they go on the errand, a "Post-it race" may be set up.

In this strategy, a pad of Post-its is mounted in a particular unobtrusive spot. The students are told privately that their job when sent as messenger is to race-walk to the Post-it pad, get one page from it and return. They are timed to see if they can accomplish this within the target time range (not running, not wandering) to earn a bonus point.

The Importance of Privacy

Management privacy is crucial to consider when developing strategies to respond to the children's special challenges. These strategies should not call attention to the children in a negative way or single them out for special treatment.

In general, this means either that things are handled with a private communication system set up when others are not around or that modifications that benefit the child with ADHD are available to classmates or siblings as well. Most teaching and management strategies that assist children who are inattentive and impulsive most of the time also benefit those who are inattentive and impulsive just some of the time.

For private communication in class, at a team practice or in the midst of playmates at home, the child is first called aside. ("Sam, I need to see you for a moment" or "Sally, I need to ask you/show you something.") Then, out of hearing of his or her peers, the child can be calmed down, reminded, encouraged, "consequenced" or taught. The send-back, audible to all, should be "Thanks!"

Now a word about "come-here's." If you've ever tried to train a dog to come, you know that it doesn't work if, whenever the dog comes in response to your call, something unpleasant happens to it.

Sometimes the most valuable come-here occurs when the child is being teased or pestered by peers or is frustrated by a task and needs a quick break or word of encouragement before he or she loses control. Let the come-here be a sign of your support and assistance, not a signal of impending doom.

Some teachers instruct a challenging student in sign language, so that quick messages can be passed between them discreetly. Others give each student a private code number or name, which it is the student's responsibility to keep private. Needless to say, the code can't be used in a way that makes it clear to whom it belongs. (Don't say, "Thirty-four, please put your hat on the floor.")

Classroom behavioral consequences are often the most embarrassing management systems of all. Imagine the respected and serious leader of a workshop on math curricula glowering at you, saying, "Mrs. Swenson's group is waiting for her to get her chin out of her hand." Names on the board, stars, achievement graphs and changing card colors announce to the world who's making it and who isn't.

Sometimes a code name or number can be utilized to give privacy to a "ticketing" color card system. For each student, a color-coded sequence of construction-paper cards moves from "excellent" to progressively less favorable colors if infractions of previously defined rules occur. Each card is associated with a particular reward or response cost. The cards are usually kept in "pockets" on a chart.

The teacher makes sure each student knows which card stack is his or hers, but doesn't know to whom the other stacks belong. When an infringement requires a card change, the teacher can just say, "Twenty-eight, talking," and change the card. Switching card numbers and location from time to time will discourage nosy students from figuring out the system.

An alternative is to keep the set of cards on the teacher's desk, out of the students' view. However, impulsive children can benefit from being able to tell at a glance what color they're on, which translates to how hard they need to work at meeting classroom rules.

The best private consequence system I've seen was that of a very caring, methodical, organized teacher. She had a classroom of some 34 extraordinarily diligent students, including several with ADHD.

Each student had a small-sized plastic margarine container with a cover on his or her desk. As students were working on their assignments, the teacher walked along in front of each student's desk, carrying a large coffee can of small plastic chips. At each desk she stopped, dipped into her can, into the child's plastic cup, and back into her can.

No one could tell which way the chips were going, or how many were changing. Her system was obviously respected by the children, who seemed aware of her watchfulness and readiness to help. They seemed to realize that they were being "caught being good."

Medication privacy is the responsibility of parent, teacher, nurse and health aid. Children can be very cruel and taunt others about their "hyper med" or "crazy pills." Systems for discreetly reminding a student to go for mid-day medication are discussed in Chapter 3.

It's important to refrain from inquiring, "Johnny, did you forget your medication this morning?" When the thought strikes you, bite your tongue, and deal with the immediate behavior. Make a note and come back to it.

Check with the parent, nurse or health aid at your next break, and decide whether the medication can be given now if it was missed and if the child can survive the classroom without its benefit—either for the time until it takes effect, or for the rest of the day if no medicine can be given. Be sure the timing of later doses is adjusted.

Conversations with, not about, the child are an important embarrassment protection, often neglected by the very professionals who should be most helpful. Sometimes parents need to tell a physician, counselor or teacher, "We need some time alone." But whenever the child is present, she or he should be specifically included in the conversation, with appropriate adjustments to the child's level of understanding and feelings.

Fitting In

Fitting in is every child's dream, the ultimate state of freedom from embarrassment. As parents and teachers, we adapt our clothing and language to fit in with our professional or social circle, but we forget how much more rigidly a child may see the requirements for fitting in.

Packaging—what children wear, how they comb their hair, how they tie their shoes—is a critical aspect of fitting in, which it is appropriate to indulge. Children who are oblivious to the packaging codes have a steeper hill to climb for social acceptability and self-esteem.

Affective matching is another fitting-in art. If you join three girls who are complaining about the math assignment, and you comment that it's fun, you lose, even if you really do think the math assignment is fun.

Even in elementary school, it's OK to speak your own mind some of the time; the art comes in choosing the moment. You can comment that math is fun when others are saying they like the teacher's jokes, but it's better to voice your complaint about the last book report when everyone else is complaining. Affective matching skill is not usually taught, but adults need to respect it as one of the subtle aspects of embarrassment protection that children will try, more or less successfully, to cultivate in their struggle for self-esteem.

Chapter 5

Enjoying the Trip: Protecting Feelings and Managing Anger

In this chapter, we're going to start with feelings and end up with action plans. The action plan, and everything that goes into it, serves as one of the best protectors of feelings and, in turn, of self-esteem. Feelings can easily get in the way of self-esteem—not only children's feelings, but also adults' feelings.

Remember that some children with ADHD are cheerful and bouncy, and others are as grumpy and negative and oppositional as you can imagine. The more a child fits the latter description, the more important this chapter is to the adults who care for her or him, since grumpy children tend to make grumpy adults, and vice versa.

If you have only gotten angry twice, you can skim the first part of this chapter. If you have never gotten angry, read on. I don't believe you.

Understanding about self-esteem and understanding about ADHD doesn't make it all better. Perhaps the biggest concern of the sensitive teacher or parent of a child with ADHD is recognizing how many times hurtful things are said in the frustration of dealing with the ADHD symptoms.

That's why we're going to talk now about *F,* feelings in general, and anger (with its related annoyance, irritability, resentment and depression) in particular. The anger makes teachers snarl, parents shout and students quit.

When intense, anger is like an emotional nausea that sometimes needs a good vomiting session to discharge the sensation. It's important to recognize nausea and get to the toilet bowl so you don't have to clean up the carpet. It's important to recognize the anger so you can let it out where it won't cause unnecessary hurt that then needs to be healed.

Anger happens. The ADHD child often elicits intense responses from parents, teachers, siblings and peers. If these responses are negative, they tend to be devastating to feelings and self-esteem. We need to learn to decrease anger and increase laughter, decrease urges to hit and increase applause, both in the child and in ourselves.

No matter how well we use the ABCD tools, negative feelings will trip us up and sour our other efforts to assist the student's self-esteem. And without self-esteem, everything stops.

Why Is Everybody Shouting?

A variety of factors contribute to the shouting:

- the symptoms of ADHD themselves
- the frustration of the child
- the reaction of the adult to the symptoms
- grieving
- the overflow of other life stresses onto the vulnerable child

Have you ever had the sense that a child was shouting just because he or she wanted to shout—and wanted you to do the same? Sometimes, it just feels good to shout.

Have you ever asked a child to do something several times—over and over, in a nice voice—and got nowhere until you shouted? Unknowingly, the child rewarded you for shouting, so you're more likely to shout again next time.

In our bike analogy, the parents were shouting to protect their son—and passers-by—from the risks of speed and poor directional control. It's not hard to imagine the boy shouting too, frustrated at the unexpected crashes and falls, and frustrated at being shouted at. If it were your bike that didn't go where you wanted it, wouldn't you sometimes want to shout at it?

Some of the shouting comes from adults' reaction to the child's problems. The child with ADHD, particularly if oppositional, can be very teacher or parent expensive. Parents speak of being resentful because their child requires so much more energy, patience, monitoring—so much more parenting—than other children. Teachers speak of burn-out and resent the time and calm taken from other students.

Parents and teachers feel good when their children or their students do well. They enjoy that reflected sense of their own ability in their parenting or teaching role.

Children with ADHD can be particularly hard on the egos of those who care for them. Whatever judgments of parents of boisterous children I may have made in my single days come back as self-judgments in my days of parenting—a truth for everyone but even more so when parenting is challenging.

Grief is one of the hidden causes of anger. The stages of grieving include denial, anger and depression. None of us ever get the child we expected. But when a child is handicapped and hurting, the disparity between the hoped-for and the real may present enough contrast that parents find themselves in a recurrent state of grief.

Finally, there are the host of adult stresses—overcrowded classrooms and tight budgets, long parent workdays and inadequate childcare, parental strife and departmental upheavals. Inhibitions may keep us from showing our anger to spouse or boss, so it all gets packed away to come spewing out when a child or student pushes the button.

Anger Risk Insurance

Anger is kind of like death. It's one of those things we don't want to talk about or admit to, but it does happen to everyone. Don't feel guilty, do something! We need an insurance plan.

Smiling at Yourself by Allen Mendler and *Am I In Trouble?* by Richard Curwin and Allen Mendler (ETR Associates, 1990) describe a number of excellent techniques for dealing with feelings and preventing problems that might escalate into anger. Their techniques, as well as others, will be mentioned here as part of a safety plan.

Take a mental picture of the following Anger Insurance House diagram and lock it into your memory where you can get to it easily. It has seven parts:

- Rest and Relaxation (window)
- Feeling Vents (chimney)
- Protection (roof)
- Insulation (attic)
- Laughter (window)
- Communication (door)
- Action Plans (steps)

Anger Insurance House

Protection

Insulation

Feeling Vents

Laughter

Rest and Relaxation

Communication

Action Plans

Rest and Relaxation

We are responsible for our own mental and physical health. Beware of becoming a martyr to your job or child. You'll resent it, and the resentment will show. The more stresses we experience, the more we need to be pro-active in our own care. You need and deserve rest, exercise and good nutrition.

Smoking, alcohol and other chemical relaxers make matters much worse. Get professional help (fast) if alcohol or other drugs seem the only way you can relax, or if you just can't relax, period.

A good spouse or friend listens and says, "Poor baby!" A good therapist can help problem solve. Just make sure the therapist understands what it means to have a child with ADHD symptoms in the classroom or at home.

A short vigorous walk can start the day on the right foot. Reserve at least an hour each week for your own thing—hobby, sport, classes, creative outlets. Make time to nurture your foundations—faith, friendships and family relationships. Learn a relaxation technique that works for you.

Check out your other life stressors, and see what you can do to make things better in other spheres. Make the opportunity to do things that give you a sense of your own competence and skill. Managing children won't necessarily do that, even if you're very competent with them.

If you are a parent, I hear you saying, "But...." I know. Your child needs constant monitoring, it's hard to find anyone else capable of handling her or him.... Do it! You *can* find someone to help.

Tell another parent you need off-duty time. Walk on your lunch hour, or get up half an hour earlier (but get to bed earlier, too). Find a teacher or student teacher who'd like to work an extra hour or two. Swap gardening for a friend (if you like to garden) or sewing (if you like to sew) for supervision of your child.

Feeling Vents

Venting anger is critical. When well done, it can release emotional energy without hurting people or property, model a technique for anger management, and even get a child's attention without hurting feelings.

When anger is not vented appropriately, it feeds resentment, irritation, annoyance and depression. It leaks out in unfairness, ridicule, disparaging comments and even abuse.

When you feel angry about a lot of things, write them all down. Then tear the note into shreds or scribble all over it. The object is to avoid hurting anyone else, so don't send it.

In *Smiling at Yourself,* Allen Mendler describes Pillow Pounding, Pillow Screaming, The Empty Chair, Towel Twisting or Biting, and Let Yourself Shake. Adults can use these techniques, too, and teach children the techniques in the process.

To vent your anger and get the child's attention at the same time, clap your hands loudly, blow a whistle, or, if you're driving in the car, momentarily turn up the radio. If the child is having problems with hitting or kicking when angry, you might want to model the "angry stomp": To show how angry you feel, put your hands on your hips and stomp your feet hard. (If you are stomping your feet with your hands on your hips, you can't be kicking and hitting.)

Protection

If you find that your students or children push you to the limit, develop a protection system, a way to escape if it's getting too hot. If you are a teacher with an aide, you may want to take a restroom break and splash water on your face, or give the aide responsibility (and appropriate tools) for working with the challenging student.

Teacher teaming. At one school, teachers in nearby classrooms teamed, so that a child acting out in one classroom would be decisively walked for "rest time" into the back of the other classroom. The teacher's face-saving communication was "Can Tom rest here? It's a bit noisy in our room." There, somewhat intimidated by the presence of students in a different grade, Tom would take his time out with some self-restraint and return to a somewhat recuperated teacher at the designated time.

Parent shifts. At home, if there are two parent figures, change shifts. At shift change, announce: "Dad's on duty now, until...." Then stick to it. All requests and arguments are deferred to him. All limits and safety precautions are his responsibility.

If this technique is to work, the off-duty parent may have to bite his or her tongue when things are done differently. No two people parent alike, and men and women almost always parent differently. I sometimes think fewer people would get divorced if they had learned how to change parenting shifts under one roof.

Reset time. When there isn't another adult around, one approach to try is "reset time," which is different from time out. The purpose of reset time is not to punish, but to provide an opportunity for child and adult to reset emotionally.

Remember that children with ADHD tend to have problems controlling emotions. They may get stuck in negative moods. They also have trouble staying in one place.

You are entitled to provide yourself with protection from the out-of-control, screaming child who follows you around the house as you desperately try to ignore the screams and stick to your decision that he or she can't have a cookie right now.

Both teacher and classmates are entitled to protection from the loud, angry arguments of a student's protest over a low grade. The child, too, deserves protection from the embarrassment of being out of control.

When a child is out of control, getting him or her back in control (and keeping yourself in control) are the issues, not punishment for the out-of-control emotions. We know that giving a child a higher grade or a cookie might calm the tears, but it's the wrong answer; it rewards being out of control. You need to be able to separate the child in a safe, calming (not necessarily punitive) place and know that he or she will stay there.

At school, the counselor's office may be a good place for reset time. The counselor can reinforce cognitive-behavioral training, helping the student use calming and "How could I handle it better next time?" strategies. Behavioral consequences for losing control may also be handled by the counselor.

At home, if the child is safe in the house, one approach is a brief parent's respite time. Announce "I'm taking reset time," go into your bedroom, lock the door if the child won't stay out, and choose your favorite venting or relaxation technique.

While the child's bedroom is not considered the best place for time out for a misdeed, it can be an appropriate place for reset time. If the raging child won't stay in the bedroom, you might develop some system that enforces, safely, the child's security in the room.

Some people enforce this policy with a single spank if the child won't stay in the room. Others use a mechanical method of securing the door if the child has demonstrated that he or she won't stay in otherwise. (A shoelace can be looped around two nails at the top of the door, one on the inside of the door itself and one on the outside of the door jam, which allows the door to be partly open but prevents escape.)

The child is allowed to holler (it's his or her throat), pound, hit (so long as there is no breakage) until the tantrum has passed. Breakage carries its own consequence.

Parents who had effectively used a reset time system for their son when he was younger were concerned that now, in fourth grade, he would run into his room whenever he was losing control. He would refuse to talk with anyone until he emerged, but he did seem to "work it all out" so that he was calm when he came out.

My comment: Job well done. Their son still has to contend with the emotional mood swings of ADHD, but he has learned a safe system that he can control.

In some cases, it is effective to hold the raging, out-of-control child until she or he calms down. However, this may involve more sensory input than the child with ADHD can handle, distressing the child further rather than helping. It may also place intolerable further emotional stress on the already at-wit's-end adult trying to hang on while the child thrashes.

Tape recording is a portable protection system. Start recording when things seem stuck or upsetting. The tape recorder helps in several ways:

- ❧ When I know I'm being recorded, I do a better job of keeping my cool and being resourceful.

- ❧ It feels good to know that I can let someone else listen to the tape so they can understand what it's like, even if I never play it again.

- ❧ The child becomes aware, too, and begins to monitor her or his own words better.

The tape can be a very helpful basis for some problem-solving work with a therapist. A tape recording can also be used in the classroom and may be the basis for subsequent problem solving in a group session with the school guidance counselor.

Insulation

Insulation is a mental protection system. Sorting, focusing and creative imagining are insulation strategies. As the child gets older, you can use these more. They are particularly important for teachers, who often can't physically escape.

Sorting involves pulling your ego (and the child's) out of danger. Realize that when children are ranting and raving or wheedling, whining and cajoling, their steering and brakes are stuck.

Their mood control is out of whack; their satisfaction center is on empty;

their vocal cords are on impulse; and they can't change gears. They don't mean to attack you, and it isn't your fault.

You probably can't get a child to stop ranting at you until the "rant" is gone, so don't try. It's just how it is, like a hot day.

Focusing means keeping your eye on the issue. Repeat only the central decision, just like a "stuck record." Avoid getting pulled into arguments by using words like "nevertheless," "regardless" and "non-negotiable." Greg Bodenhamer's excellent book *Back in Control* (Prentice Hall, 1987) has more discussion of this technique.

When the why questions keep coming or the arguments escalate, you respond with "Nevertheless, I said...." If the child doesn't seem to hear you, try saying, "You asked me a question. I gave you an answer. What was my answer?"

Imagining is giving yourself a mental escape valve. It may give you a chuckle and help you get things back in perspective. Imagine the wiggly five year old all dressed for work, briefcase in hand, when you're trying to figure out why she or he won't be reasonable.

Imagine the first time you held your infant in your arms—not so very long ago—with those perfect tiny fingernails, the face wrinkling in the light. Remember that she or he is, after all, a child in need of nurture, not just a terrible force to be contended with.

Imagine yourself relaxing at your favorite activity or non-activity in some pleasant spot. Take a minute vacation. If you're teaching children to use Guided Pictures, Breathing for Relaxation, or Relaxing Your Whole Body (techniques from *Smiling at Yourself*), you might try one of these techniques yourself.

Laughter

Laughter is a wonderful way to get away from the shouting. *Am I In Trouble?* includes an excellent discussion of humor's use in discipline.

Bikes and Baboons, Plane Crash, The Misplaced Meal, Bait and Switch, the Whine-In and The Riot Act are excellent examples.

As the authors caution, however, humor in discipline needs to be used with care. The humor shouldn't reward negative behavior, shouldn't be confusing and shouldn't make children feel they are being laughed at.

Silliness and joy are first cousins of humor. They can be freely laced through interactions with children and are part of the celebration of being around children.

Winner's Stunts is a silly reward system. Put some pieces of paper in a basket. On each paper, write a stunt that the adult will do if the child or children win. Some examples: stand on one foot saying "Mary Had a Little Lamb," do jumping jacks, or pretend to be a marionette.

Sometimes some "special service" rewards can be included. For example, a teacher or parent might volunteer to clean the child's desk. Children love to have a part in making up the papers—but the adult does get to remove any suggestions that are too wild.

Rita is a professional friend of mine who never grew up. Or at least, she hasn't stopped playing with children. She spends time with her four children for fun. When one of her four is grumpy and oppositional, she smiles or chuckles warmly and grumps right back.

She does this in a way that says, "I love you; you look funny when you grump." The egos are safe. No buttons are being pushed. The relationship is supportive, and she's providing a handle of love and laughter for the child to take hold of to pull herself or himself out of the grumps.

Communication

Communication is a topic in itself. To keep track of the aspects of communication, store a mental image of the Y-Man, standing in the doorway of the Anger Insurance House already in your memory. In particular, remember the "Y" when a child asks "Why?"

Communication involves *active attending* (eyes and ears), *current comments* (mouth), *help with feelings* (emotional eyebrows), *teaming* (heart-head), *democratic discussions* (Y-Man's trunk), *just judgments* (right or left arm), and *firm follow-through* (action legs).

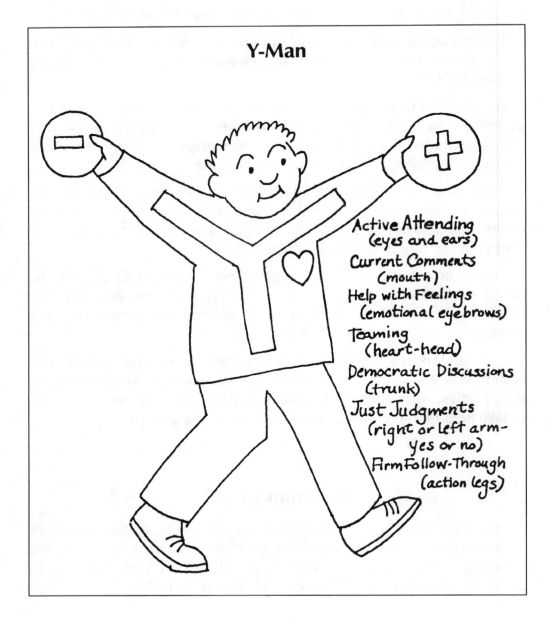

Y-Man

Active Attending
(eyes and ears)
Current Comments
(mouth)
Help with Feelings
(emotional eyebrows)
Teaming
(heart-head)
Democratic Discussions
(trunk)
Just Judgments
(right or left arm—
yes or no)
Firm Follow-Through
(action legs)

Active Attending

Active attending involves stopping, looking and listening to a child's universal needs and present actions, feelings and thoughts. It's noticing that a child is in the middle of a good show (which she or he had permission to watch) before asking the child to clean her or his room "now." It's realizing that the child is watching the snow falling before you ask him or her to solve a math problem, realizing that the child is "starving" before you ask for the homework assignment, realizing that medication has worn off before you punish the child for standing while he or she works.

Current Comments

Current comments arise out of your awareness of the child's present state, with attentive non-judgmental observations. I-statements always help:

- ❧ I have trouble thinking about math when it's beginning to snow.

- ❧ I'd find that bookbag heavy to carry.

- ❧ I like dinosaur shirts.

When initiating a conversation, avoid interrogations and comments about a different time or place. When children get home from school, they probably aren't thinking about school if they can help it. "What did you do today?" takes them back to where they just escaped from.

Jumping on a child with a list of "all the things we have to do today" is also not a good way to bridge communication. Some researchers feel that the oppositional response of children with ADHD to communication that imposes our time, place, schedule or question may be self-defense. These children already have enough trouble keeping track of their own thoughts.

Be wary of the undone compliment. For example: "Why can't you always do it that way?" "Wouldn't it be great if we could always have such a good time?" Resentment has contaminated these comments. Remember that the one constant outcome of steering problems and speed spurts is inconsistency. Let the child enjoy the good results when they happen.

Overly effusive praise, however, can be perceived as a value judgment, implying a criticism of other times even without reference to them. "Wow, this is outstanding writing," may be a bit too much, especially if you're feeling "why not always" as you say it. A simple "Nice!" or "This is fun!" works well.

Help with Feelings

For help with feelings, remember the following three phrases:

- Name, claim, aim.
- KISS, or Keep It Short and Simple.
- Reach out and touch someone.

My most vivid experience with **Name, Claim, Aim** occurred when I was examining a four year old. The child bumped into a small lightweight wall-hanging that slipped off and insulted him, landing on his head and shoulder. He exploded, pounding the wall, grabbing for the nails, looking as though he would tear the fabric or the balsa frame.

My first response, to reach to restrain him, was met with intensification of the wildness. Stopping to heed my own teachings, I then said, "It was mean of that frame to fall on you! It would make me feel very angry." *(Name it.)* "Show me how angry you feel." *(Claim it.)* With that I lifted him down from the exam table to stand in front of my desk, handed him a paper and pencil, and invited him to show me on the paper. *(Aim it.)*

He began by drawing one very dark line. When I assured him that what happened would have made me much angrier than that, he resumed with a great deal of furious scribbling, which gradually slowed as the energy was vented. Within a minute, it was all over. Some of the venting ideas discussed earlier are good ways to aim a child's anger as well as our own.

KISS is important for wordy people like me who like to lecture. Fewer words are better: "What a bummer." "That would make me angry." "How frustrating."

Reach out and touch, physically or with a sign, the child who can't hear you. A child ranting and raving in her or his room with self-negating comments may be "touched" by a heart scribbled on a piece of paper and shoved under the door. A hand squeeze may be all the communication necessary in the face of a disappointment.

Some children with ADHD are very sensitive to some types of touch and may withdraw from a light or surprising touch. On the other hand, backrubs, in an appropriate context, seem to be pleasant for many of them.

Teaming

Teaming to solve problems is negotiation strategy. The problems are put on the table and the adult and child sit on the same side of the table to solve the problem.

I-statements are the invitation to team:

- ✺ I feel confused when I look at your desk. I wonder if we could think of a good desk-straightening game.

- ✺ I feel disappointed putting a zero down for you when your assignment doesn't get turned in. I'd like to know of a good system to get those papers back to my desk after all the work you do to finish them.

You-statements and overgeneralizations interfere, attack and invite argument and counter-attack:

- ✺ Your desk is always disorganized. Why can't you figure out how to keep it in better order?

- ✺ You never get your assignments turned in. Why can't you just get them up to my desk?

You can imagine the responses to comments like these.

Once you've clearly put yourself on the same team with the child and put the problem on the table, problem-solve. Brainstorming, considering options and possible outcomes, contracts and action plans are good teamwork tools. Remember, you're on the same team!

Democratic Discussions and Just Judgments

These make up the Y of our Y-Man. Please take a moment right now to make a Y, using your arm for the trunk and your index and middle finger for the branches, folding the other fingers down. This is a major emergency communication tool. You need your Y with you at all times.

The trunk of the Y, your forearm, is the democratic discussion. Make sure it always comes before, and never after, the just judgment represented by one of the fingers. In a court of law, the two sides present their case first (democratic discussion). Then the just judgment is made. The lawyers go home after that.

As parents and teachers, we keep getting it backwards, and end up in trouble. A child asks us for a favor. We say no (a judgment), and then the discussion—or argument—begins.

Bright children with ADHD tend to be phenomenal arguers. Their tenacity, insatiability and creativity help them come up with the most ingenious arguments.

These arguments combine with the risk of emotional escalation as a final catastrophic consequence if the child doesn't get her or his way. Children can end up winning a lot of arguments as long as adults remain convinced that judgment followed by debate is the way it's done.

Listen to yourself the next time you make a request of the child (a judgment for action) or answer a plea. Did you ask the lawyers to present their cases first or allow them to argue afterward?

Discussion-first openers could include:

- ❧ The room needs to be cleaned. Do you want to do it now or as soon as the program ends?

꙲ I think I know what my decision will be (about giving an extra day for the assignment or going out for pizza tonight), but tell me your thoughts first.

Once you've heard and know you won't be willing to hear any more discussion, state your judgment (yes or no, one finger or the other), be clear that your decision is final, and stick to it. Now you may need to use insulation techniques.

Firm Follow-Through

The action legs of Y-Man stand for the *firm follow-through,* essential for making your requests happen. When you have made a decisive request, stay to see that it is done. For example: "The show's over. Now it's time to pick up your room." "The assignment's due tomorrow. I'll watch you do the first problem." If compliance is not prompt, be with the child to walk her or him through completion.

This is not just good control, but good teaching. When one father began to follow-through with his son on cleaning his room, the father realized that the boy didn't know how to get shirts to stay on the hanger, which was why he never hung them up.

Follow-through is even more important in the classroom. When students aren't succeeding with requests or assignments, walk them through each step to find out where they are stuck.

Action Plans

Have you ever noticed that you start to shout when you can't think of anything else to do in a situation? That's where an action plan can help. Action plans are the final concept in our home insurance plan, the front steps of the house.

The action plan is made in advance of an expected situation, so you can quickly fall back on it when the situation arises. Let's look at the steps for developing an action plan.

1. **Choose a single problem.**

   - the most bothersome (it drives you crazy)

   - the most dangerous (running into the street)

   - the most important (hitting is not allowed)

2. **Clarify it.**

   - What leads up to it? When could intervention start?

   - When does it start (exactly)? Could medication be wearing off at the time?

   - With whom? Is someone else's strategy already working?

   - How often? Is it habit or a rare event?

   - What is the child feeling? Can you help with his or her comfort level and control?

   - What are you feeling? Does your ego need some insulation?

   - What has been tried? Don't keep using a recipe that's failed.

3. **Choose tools from those discussed—ABCDEF, Esteem Kid, Anger Insurance House and Y-Man.**

   - Adaptations—making success more likely

   - Behavior management strategies—rules and results

   - Cognitive-behavioral training—lessons in self-control

   - Diagnosing, demystifying and drug therapy modification

   - Esteem—feeling valued, in control, capable and protected from embarrassment

   - Feelings management—rest and relaxation, vents, protection, insulation, laughter and communication

- Y-Man—active attending, current comments, help with feelings, teaming, democratic discussions, just judgments and firm follow-through

4. Determine your action plan.

In most cases, a few problem situations tend to recur often. Go after those situations with an action plan. When you are caught off guard, use the tools and techniques we've discussed—ABCDEF, Esteem Kid, the Anger Insurance House and Y-Man—to help you find an on-the-spot solution.

If you get stuck, get an objective third party to help you decide what are musts and what are maybes, what you can do after all the "buts" are considered and resolved. Many families need an outsider's help with teamwork.

Let's try developing action plans for a whiny passenger and for an aggressive student.

Action Plan for a Whiny Passenger

Problem choice: The five-year-old daughter starts begging for something when she and Mom are in the car and just won't quit, long after Mom says no. The family chooses this problem to work on because it's very bothersome to Mom, and it may be a traffic hazard.

What leads up to it? The child asks for a special treat when out on errands with Mom and won't accept no for an answer. The begging sometimes begins before they leave the house and doesn't end until they're home. Sounds like intervention better start at home.

How about a behavioral contract—one star (Mom carries them with her) for every five minutes of pleasure on errands and one grab from the Winner's Stunt basket if the daughter can earn at least four stars? Or Mom could use colored sticks for ticketing correction, with a stunt at home if the daughter gets only two sticks moved to the "whoops" pocket.

When does it start (exactly)? Mom usually does errands before she picks up the older brother from school at 3:30 p.m., so the problem occurs between 2:00 and 3:30 p.m. Is this almost naptime? Is Ritalin wearing off from the 11:00 a.m. dose in a young child who metabolizes medication rapidly?

Some adaptations may be in order. Would it be better to get errands done earlier, perhaps right after lunch, while the medication is working and before the child is so tired?

With whom? Dad says there's no problem. On his errands on Saturday mornings, the children take turns going with him. His errands are usually shorter than Mom's. Hmmm, another possible adaptation—shorter errands, done in the morning? (Except Mom doesn't have time earlier....)

How often? It's a pretty regular problem for Mom—at least twice weekly. Sounds like help is needed.

What is the child feeling? Tired, low on medicine, restless and insatiable. She was in kindergarten in the morning. Maybe she's feeling Mom uses the time with her for errands and then everything starts happening for big brother after that.

Attend to the child's feelings. It's hard for a five year old to discuss her frustration, but Mom can put some extra energy into making her feel special on the trip.

Adapt by changing the time and planning errands that include a special treat for the child, maybe not so many at a time. The treat might be a stop to swing at the park or to blow some bubbles. Given the insatiability, it may be impossible to go shopping where there's anything the child thinks she'd like.

How about Y-Man? Some communication discussion might be possible here, even at age five. "You want something special to happen when we go on errands. You choose a treat for today." (A limited number of choices keeps the girl involved but not overwhelmed.) Knowing she had the discussion may make it easier for Mom to stick to her just judgment.

What are you feeling? Mom is feeling in the red—furious, frazzled and frustrated. If nothing works and it gets too bad, she'll need a vent. Now's the time to suddenly turn up the car radio very loud.

How about laughing? Can Mom get the daughter giggling with an echo or by commanding her not to smile?

Insulation would certainly be worth a try. Sort—get the ego unhooked. Focus—stuck record, nevertheless, regardless of all arguments, don't give an extra treat because she's whining.

Does Mom have her Y-Man ready? She's had the democratic discussion. Now she needs to follow-through on her just judgment. Still arguing? Time for imagination.

Who is this tiny lawyer sitting next to Mom? Surely a child prodigy? And only five years ago she was so tiny and sticky. How did she find time for law school?

It would be nice if she'd polish her presentation, a little less of the melodrama maybe. Time to leave her to her lawyering and mentally check into a friendly spa.

That's how you do an action plan. These are the tools we've used:

- *Adaptations*—shorter errands, done earlier.

- *Behavior management strategies*—star or stick system plus Winner's Stunt basket.

- *Cognitive-behavioral training*—Just for Mom, the child's too young. But Mom's doing great—she should reward herself.

- *Drug therapy modification*— At the next visit to the physician, remember to ask if the medicine might be wearing off in three hours instead of four. Meanwhile, adapt the shopping schedule to allow for that possibility.

- *Esteem*—Mom is valuing the daughter as she hears her needs. She is helping her feel capable and in control by asking her to choose which treats she wants and setting up a behavioral system with clear rules and short intervals so success is likely.

> *Feelings*—Mom identified and respected her daughter's and will take care of her own with clear Y-Man communication and the options of vents, insulation and laughter.

Action Plan for an Aggressive Student

Problem choice: Seven-year-old Jerry is physically aggressive at school and sometimes elsewhere with large groups of children. Jerry's aggression is important, potentially dangerous and bothersome. Hitting, kicking, scratching and biting may be experiments in two-year-old autonomy. They may also be the impulsive reactions of a teased and frustrated child, but they are not acceptable social behaviors.

What leads up to it? Jerry seems to hit if he's teased or if someone bumps into him (even if it's accidental).

It may be helpful to have some cognitive-behavioral training on handling teasing, sensing when and why he's getting upset, and learning the power of the "Thanks!" response to teasing. Stop-think and relaxation strategies may help.

Get in touch with the school guidance counselor or another mental health professional who can help with these strategies. Meanwhile in the classroom, the teacher can work on improving classroom relations (see the section on Membership in Chapter 6).

When does it start (exactly)? Could medication be wearing off at the time? For Jerry, the hour of the day seems to vary, but he had been better for several months and has gotten worse over the past two months. Teacher, family and after-school care providers should consider some of the following factors:

- Increased stresses at home or school

- Escalating embarrassments, making him more vulnerable to teasing

- Medication change (perhaps changing to generic from brand name) or medication tolerance. Sometimes such a change coincides with the change to daylight savings time, when sleep schedules become disrupted and chronic fatigue sets in.

Parents and teachers should examine and care for their own stresses and try to problem-solve those areas that directly involve the child. Reassess the medication choice and level.

With whom? Jerry has difficulty in his regular classroom but has not had difficulty in art or soccer. He does not generally have difficulty at home.

Before assuming that the teacher's techniques are inferior, check to see if the difficulty is always with the same one or two students. If that is the case, group work by the school guidance counselor with the three students may be very helpful.

Realize that the classroom may be Jerry's most embarrassing and most vulnerable setting. If he is excellent at art and soccer, his successes there may be protective.

The classroom teacher may need to offer more "fresh potato chip" attention and more sensitive embarrassment protection. Jerry also needs a very clear no-hitting policy, backed by positive and negative behavioral interventions, enforced by both teacher and parents.

It's time for esteem-protecting "goof insurance." The teacher should seek to prevent situations where Jerry's aggression may erupt.

Close supervision and instruction in non-physical means of dealing with differences can help. The teacher also needs to help Jerry avoid guaranteed trouble situations for restless, impulsive children, such as standing in line or sitting close to others in circle time.

How often? It has been occurring several times a week, which suggests serious distress. Intervention needs to be intense and immediate.

What is the child feeling? Jerry's aggression appears to be an immediate reaction to perceived insults from others. (This is different from the rare child with a more profound disorder who seems to find pleasure in hurting animals and people. That child needs psychiatric assistance.)

When bumped, Jerry's poor sensory sorting and lack of reflection may register the contact as "Intentional hit, defend," rather than "Accident, no response needed." He may get emotionally "stuck" when he begins to feel bad, getting angrier than the situation deserves with little ability to get himself back into control.

If Jerry has been watching television programs that model aggressive interactions as "heroic," his defensive impulse is likely to be aggressive. If his self-esteem is particularly low, he may be feeling that everyone is against him anyway.

He may also be particularly sensitive to teasing and need to demonstrate that he's a "super-hero." He may think this is what a parent's admonition to learn to stand up for himself means.

These vulnerabilities do not mean that Jerry should be spared the appropriate consequences of his actions. But he does need stronger behavioral motivators to stay in control, a chance for emotional resetting when he is out of control, and energetic "feelings management."

Behavioral intervention should be initiated promptly to control the aggressive behavior, using a combination of response cost, reward, and reset or time out. Parent-teacher teaming is critical. (Suggestions for specific behavioral and emotional interventions for Jerry are listed later in this action plan.)

What are you feeling? Teachers and parents are probably feeling some sense of failure in their respective skills. They may also feel some degree of blame for each other, as well as dismay, disappointment and anger at Jerry.

Their unrelated upsets may have contributed to some of the emotional intensity Jerry is experiencing. They need to take a good look at the Anger Insurance House and use whatever techniques they need to take care of themselves so that they can get back to constructive communication with Jerry.

What has been tried? The old recipes for Jerry were grounding and loss of television rights. He is already grounded and has been forbidden to watch television for the next three weeks—so there is no immediate ammunition left, no way for him to get out of the doghouse.

He has lost his one healthful activity, biking, so he is in an escalating cycle of anger and alienation. The punishments are not a useful method this time. Let's look more carefully at specific behavioral and feeling strategies to use now.

1. There must be a clear statement that aggression—physical contact that is meant to bother or hurt another person—cannot be accepted. Period. A child with ADHD cannot deal with subtle qualifications, such as, "But don't let anyone push you around—stand up for yourself and fight back."

2. Define appropriate alternate behaviors. Such behaviors may include:

   ❧ Saying "Thanks" as a response to teasing.

   ❧ Stamping feet and clapping hands when angry.

   ❧ Reporting to a supervising adult if he is being pestered or injured.

   ❧ Learning the kinds of avoidance strategies taught in aikido.

3. Define predictable consequences, such as the following:

   ❧ Reward for non-aggression: For each day that Jerry does not exhibit physical aggression toward anyone, he should be given special extra time with a parent. In general, this time is most exciting for a child if it is with the father, because he is generally less available to the child. Special activities may include going for a walk together, extra story time, the father doing jumping jacks. This special time is lost by the first infraction of the non-physical aggression rule each day.

   ❧ Reward for using an alternate behavior: This reward should happen immediately. It could be a privately understood comment and a credit marked on his daily reporting form or the class "bonus page." If the teacher catches him stamping his feet and clapping his hands or saying "thanks" in response to teasing, the teacher can say "dinosaurs" (or whatever word they've agreed on) to no one in particular and mark the credit. The credits for the points may be "cashed in" within the framework of a home or school reward system. Remember that rewards are part of cognitive-behavioral training, too.

- Immediate time out is a logical consequence of any physical aggression. Time out is indicated immediately for any hurtful aggression. A minute per year of age is recommended. The time may need to be even shorter for children who have great difficulty with attentional focus and movement control.

- If Jerry is completely out of control, reset time is used until he has had a chance to calm down before time out or another logical consequence is used.

- Response cost during time out (after reset time) may involve writing (or telling a tape recorder) what happened and two or three ways he could handle a similar situation without hitting or kicking the next time. This logical consequence lets him vent (by telling what happened) but then moves him forward to constructive problem solving. Asking Jerry to write a letter of apology sounds very civilized, but it assumes all the fault is his. Such an approach is likely to aggravate anger and lower self-esteem. Mutual apologies, on the other hand, are always appropriate.

- A private word may signify the "ticketing" using the classroom's system—turning of his card color or loss of classroom credits. At home, it might signify a mark that will mean he won't get to play with a friend that day.

4. Feelings management for Jerry includes:

- Avoiding television violence (including many cartoons).

- Avoiding physical punishment, such as spanks or swats and roughhousing, which blur the issues.

- Giving "legal" outlets for frustration and anger (such as talking or writing about it, scribbling how angry he feels on cardboard, or pounding a punching bag).

- Advocating for him in unnecessarily frustrating situations.

- At home, indulging him with cuddling, bedtime tuck-in routines, and backrubs to help him relax.

- Providing more opportunities for him to demonstrate his skills in ways that will gain peer as well as adult approval, and commenting positively when he does well.

- Considering an "adopt a student" program at the school and including Jerry in it if his family is unable to provide him with much emotional support.

In summary, the tools used to solve Jerry's aggression include:

- *Adaptations*—closer monitoring, interventions to decrease teasing by others, and avoidance of close physical proximity to the other involved students.

- *Behavior management strategies*—a parent-teacher consensus statement that includes clear definition of positive behaviors to be rewarded as well as negative behavior to be avoided. The statement should also include a clear statement of rewards and logical consequences. The follow-through should be matter-of-fact. It should be done as privately as feasible in public settings.

- *Cognitive-behavioral training*—Jerry needs to understand the problematic situations and his degree of responsibility for them. He should be trained in stop-think, teasing and anger management, and aikido avoidance techniques.

- *Drug therapy modifications*—Possible changes should be discussed with the physician. Note if there has been a change in medication, dose or brand. Make sure Jerry's been taking the medication.

- *Esteem*—Family, teacher and possibly school staff will be seeking to increase Jerry's opportunities to experience success. They should also help protect him from embarrassment and offer supportive listening and interactions that show Jerry he is valued.

- *Feelings*—Everyone's feelings (parents, teacher, Jerry and the classmates teasing him) will be explored and addressed, and communication bridges will be improved. The school guidance counselor and non-school mental health professionals may be helpful. Their assistance may be necessary if the situation does not respond to this action plan within several weeks' time.

Chapter 6

ROADS
to Classroom Success

Putting a child with ADHD in a classroom is similar to asking an athelete to take that wonderful bike with the loose steering and brakes on a bike marathon. Everyone is supposed to take off at the same time, follow the same path, and get safely to the end of course in some reasonable time. Imagine the frustration of fellow riders, and the rider of the special bike, as that bike with a directional difference and hyperspeed bumps into the other bikes, veers erratically back and forth across the flow of traffic, and sometimes fails to stop at stop signs.

If the course involves any winding, narrow paths, the odds are that the bike with ADHD is going to repeatedly veer completely off the route. The rider probably won't be able to steer it to the end of the course at all. And yet, if the course were a broad, straight, uphill boulevard, the rider of that same bike might come in first.

The teacher has the challenge of both setting the path for the educational marathon and coaching along the way. The curriculum just tells you the city for the marathon and where the marathon needs to end.

There are as many special considerations as there are students in the class. Thus, the main roads chosen need to accommodate as many of the participants as possible. Special bypass routes may be necessary to straighten the path for some special children in some areas. When designing or coaching, think back through all the ABCDEF tools: adaptations, behavior management strategies, cognitive-behavioral training, diagnosis and drug therapy, esteem building and feelings management.

This chapter describes some routes that are particularly appropriate in dealing with impulsivity and inattention, whether due to neurologic ADHD or some of the many secondary causes discussed in Appendix B. It primarily outlines ABC tools (adaptations, behavior management strategies and cognitive-behavioral training techniques), but consideration of drug therapy (when used), esteem and feelings are required foundations.

The ideas in this chapter have come from a wide range of sources, including many classroom observations. The techniques suggested should make for a more successful experience for everyone and help nourish the self-esteem of every child.

These ideas are easy to use and appropriate for the whole classroom. In some cases, special attention is drawn to children with ADHD, generally only if they have already drawn attention to themselves. In other cases, special adaptations are recommended, where it would be inappropriate or impossible for the whole class to take the bypass route that the ADHD child clearly requires.

To help you to locate or recall the recommendations in this chapter that are pertinent to the problems you are trying to solve, the outline follows the word ROADS. Let's look at the outline before embarking on this journey:

- *R* represents initial **Restructuring** of the classroom—the region where the child works (her or his desk), the classroom routines, and rules with associated rewards and consequences. As you consider these adaptations and behavior management strategies, remember the importance of preserving students' self-esteem. Then select the appropriate changes for your classroom, and set aside time to make the necessary arrangements.

- *O* is for **Organization**. Help students deal with classroom organizational demands by teaching them how to organize. Guide students in organizing their materials, assignments and paperwork. Teach them organizational strategies for developing their ideas and approaching assigned tasks. Remember to MAP IT—materials, assignments, paperwork, ideas and tasks—to help your students organize.

  Organization can be taught and graded, using a cognitive-behavioral approach. Students are rewarded for the process of using the organizational steps, independent of outcome.

- *A* is the core—**Attention**. Think of attention as having five Ts: Adaptations in teaching techniques can help *transition, tackle, tether* and *tickle* the students' attention. In some cases they also *transform* the usual curriculum with needed modifications.

  The techniques that will be discussed benefit every student whose attention has ever wandered. They assist students in changing from one subject to another (transition), coming to attention (tackle), staying attentive (tether) and paying attention to the most important things (tickle). In some cases, it is necessary to transform teaching to provide some bypass routes for the more severe attentional limitations of the child with ADHD.

- **D** is for ***Dealing with Other Difficulties***. Some students need help to regulate their momentum, movement and moods. Many will have some problems with memory. The goal is to optimize the child's sense of magnificence and membership in the class. We must also be alert to medication issues.

- **S** is for **Share the Load**. Sharing is critical for the care of your feelings and the child's. Sharing the load ensures that a child receives individualized assessment and assistance that cannot take place in the classroom and that challenges beyond school are addressed. The school study team, the student's parents, and outside professionals including the child's physician, are all important players.

Now, ready, set, go—on to ROADS.

R—Restructuring

O—Organization

A—Attention

D—Dealing with Other Difficulties

S—Share the Load

Restructuring

How would you feel if you had season tickets to the theater and found that you were seated with your back to the stage, that the actors and actresses kept their voices low to avoid disturbing the adjoining theater, and that workers were running back and forth beyond the open back door that you are facing? Seems pretty bizarre, doesn't it? What if, in addition, some members of the audience were chatting or coughing during much of the performance?

How do the season-ticket holders in your classroom fare? Classrooms are not the same as theaters, for the children are not passive observers. But as teacher you are manager and director, and when you are presenting information, you are acting. If you think some restructuring might improve the "box-office" of learning for your classroom, read on.

In the Classroom

Arrange your room so that students with ADHD are more likely to be attracted to you and their books than to other social, visual and auditory magnets. Design seating with the care that an architect uses to design a theater.

Arrange the desks so that all of the students directly face the wall used for instruction, and minimize visual distractions on that wall. Sit in each seat to make sure every student can clearly see you and the board. Provide pathways to permit you to walk among the students; your presence at desk-side is very focusing. Optimize comfort with attention to lighting and room temperature. (A fan can be helpful in hot weather and may help drown out distractions when the students are doing seat-work. Just make sure it doesn't drown out your voice.)

Do small group teaching at the side or rear of the class, so you will be less distracting to those doing seat-work. Use a chalkboard (get a portable one if necessary), or have each student use a magic slate so students can chorus responses in writing, when possible, to decrease noise.

One teacher with a number of distractible children in a regular classroom has arranged all of the desks around the periphery of the room. The desks face outward and are divided by study carrels made of cardboard boxes. The students turn their chairs around for classwide information. For group instruction, students and teacher gather on the floor in a central area protected on three sides by low bookshelves.

If you use cooperative learning, where students are encouraged to do peer group work, distinguish between teacher instruction and group work time by having the students turn their chairs around so they are facing the right person at the right time.

Students must be facing you to pay attention to you. (Other children directly across the table are much stronger magnets than a teacher who is standing further away and behind the student.) If cooperative learning is used less than 50 percent of the time, have the desks face you the rest of the time, and give the students transition time to move into clusters at cooperative learning time.

Loft or open classrooms (large rooms housing several classes with minimal intervening barriers) should be avoided for students with ADHD, but if this is what you have, here are some suggestions.

Position the class with its side rather than its back or front nearest the corridor. Angle the desks nearest the corridor toward the opposite side of the room. Be sure that neither teacher nor students are in a corridor.

Extend the barriers between classes to at least seven feet in height; use a full room divider if possible. Team with home and school and private organizations in the community to acquire proper room dividers as quickly as possible.

If self-contained classrooms are available around the loft rooms, use them for any didactic presentations. Coordinate with other teachers in the loft to ensure that quiet and noisy activities coincide for all classes. Alternately, consider team teaching, and rearrange the area so the open space is used exclusively for seat-work, with assistance provided by one of the teachers or aides, while other teachers have formal sessions in the quiet rooms.

At the Desk

Try to avoid singling out students with ADHD for isolated seating. Seat them within the general classroom arrangement, but near the front of the class, facing the teacher. Avoid areas near small-group activities, the door, the pencil sharpener and windows. Some teachers prefer that the student with ADHD sit to one side rather than in the middle of the front row, so that some restless movement can be allowed without undue distraction to other students.

One teacher achieved uncluttered desktops in her class in the following manner. Desks were cleared as a requirement for going out to recess. As she escorted her students in from recess, she handed each child a pencil and a quarter page of paper. On one side of the page was the math problem, which students were to be able to solve by the time the teacher finished giving the class lesson.

With no paper shuffle, the lesson began with all students paying attention to her exciting presentation as soon as they were seated. When the students mastered the single problem, they turned over the paper to find the assignment, with page number and book name, in case they had trouble finding it on the board and weren't paying attention when she said it.

Keep no more at the desk than can be kept organized. All other materials should be in a cubby or file box. Some teachers provide several spare desks, to which students can come with just the materials needed for the single lesson to escape their own clutter.

Distractions can be buffered by seating calm, well-focused children near students with ADHD, and with study carrels or privacy boards. I have been in a number of classrooms where teachers or families have provided collapsible privacy boards for each student in the room, made with two or three panels of heavy cardboard or light presswood.

In some classrooms, students stand up a large, undecorated three-ring binder to give some visual shelter to their work. During seat-work time, auditory distractions can be buffered with a fan, earplugs (though these annoy many students with ADHD) or with earphones at a listening center.

In a reading group with two very impulsive children among fifteen students, one teacher had all the students seated around a long table (a circular table would have been better, but wasn't available). The students with ADHD were seated immediately to her right and left, so that she could use her touch to help refocus or quiet them and have them directly involved in demonstrations.

Scheduling for Success

Predictable schedules decrease the number of "sharp turns" and "sudden stops" required of the student with ADHD. They enhance the child's sense of control and mastery. When special events are expected, explain the plans well in advance, with frequent reminders.

Post schedules of daily routines. (Some students will do well if the schedule is taped on their desks.) Schedule more intensive study early in the day. Provide frequent brief breaks for movement and relaxation.

Avoid requiring the child with ADHD to do focused seat-work while other students are engaged in group activities, unless she or he is physically protected from distraction from the others. During any one time period, schedule all quiet or all noisy activities, not both kinds at once.

If a child is on medication for ADHD, recognize the special timing issues. The four-hour, short-acting Ritalin may wear off before lunch and not be effective for the first 15 to 30 minutes after a noon dose. The longer-acting medicines may take a while to become effective in the morning and may wear off before the end of the day. The prescribed timing for medication is important. Communicate with home if problems with medication timing seem to affect classroom behavior.

Rules and Rewards

Choose only a few rules (no more than five) that are worth enforcing, and do so. Wherever possible, make positive rather than negative statements. Introduce the rules clearly and sternly on the first day of class, when students are most ready to listen. Post the rules, and have students review them daily. Follow through immediately and fairly with enforcement, before anger develops.

Have clearly predictable, logical and non-emotional response-cost consequences for rule infractions. Try to avoid embarrassing the rulebreaker. Costs can include the following:

- immediate loss of a misused object (but let it be reclaimed, for home use only, after an appropriate period of time, unless it is dangerous)
- time-out teaming with another classroom
- color card system with assigned numbers to keep it private
- private non-accumulation of bonus credits

Focus student energies on reward systems. Raffle tickets or plastic chips, privately given and cashed in at a weekly assembly or class store can reward positive behaviors. Bonus academic credits can reward positive work habits.

Add marbles to a marble jar or chart the rising color on a thermometer for classwide rewards. Give group good-behavior bonus points for individual and group kindness and generosity as well as obedience.

Class rewards could include a visit to a museum, park or play; a special video; or a track meet when the goal is reached. Remember to have enough "crisp potato chips" for good performance that the soggy chips for bad behavior won't be appealing.

Contracts may help when a child with ADHD is stuck. Team with the child to develop the contract. The child must perceive that she or he is struggling. Begin by identifying feelings: "I feel sad when your card goes to red. I wonder how it feels for you."

Clarify the problem, put it on the table and sit side by side on the same team: "It sounds like your anger brake sometimes doesn't work, and you end up crashing through and hitting someone. Then, even though someone else may have started it by teasing, you get in trouble. That sounds like a bummer. How could we work together so your arm wouldn't crash through the 'no hitting sign' even when that anger brake isn't so good?"

Discuss suggestions for motivating rewards and consequences. Draw up a contract that offers frequent opportunities for success. The contract must be combined with guidance in strategies to reach success (stop-think, relaxation, and anger recognition and management). The guidance counselor can often offer invaluable assistance in contract development.

Organization

Disorganization is a natural tendency for most of us, but for some it is more natural than others. Although disorganization is very natural for children with ADHD, it is also difficult for them to function in the midst of disorganization, which complicates the problem.

Materials

Desks, books and papers need organizing. Set aside time each day for students to reorder their desks, notebooks and bookbags. Provide specific guidelines for maintaining a neat desk. Children with ADHD are particularly unable to deal with the clutter that so readily accumulates around them.

Dr. Clare Jones, an educational consultant for students with learning and attentional challenges, recommends color-coding classroom subjects. Give each subject a different color, and use that color throughout the year. Have students keep a colored folder (with pockets for worksheets, which may also be color-coded) for each subject. Put a matching colored sticker on the front of the associated notebooks and texts, and keep them all together inside the folder.

A box can be used as a portable file to help students who lose papers in their desks. (If space permits, this option should be available to all students.) Keep the colored folders, open edge up, in the box for easy access and storage.

Assignments

It is astonishing how many parents report that they have witnessed their children complete assignments that are never turned in. Students with ADHD seem likely to be on a trip to Mars when the assignment is given, out to lunch when they should have been packing their books to take home, and out of sorts at homework time.

To have actually done the homework but failed to turn it in seems incredible. But there indeed are those papers, crumpled in the bottom of the bookbag, stuffed into a different book, or coming out of a pants pocket on the other side of the wash, testifying to the appropriateness of the zero in the teacher's grade book. A system for organizing homework can help.

For all homework assignments in lower grades, a simple color-coded homework folder is recommended, consisting of a front pocket (To Home), a back pocket (To School) and a central area into which a supply of weekly assignment sheets are fastened. Younger students and those with ADHD tend to be impatient with three-ring notebooks and dividers (they prefer to stuff and yank). Simpler is better. Whether this folder or a three-ring binder is used, instruct in and reward its proper use.

If the teacher can predict all assignments on a weekly or monthly basis, all students and parents will benefit from a copy of the assigment schedule.

An easily used assignment sheet lists the usual types of assignments down the left-hand column (math workbook, math text, spelling, language worksheet, etc.), with some spaces for variations. The bottom two rows are open for teacher and parent signatures and comments. The sheet has columns for Monday through Friday assignments. With this system, students (and parents) are reminded of the usual assignments, but are only

Sample Assignment Sheet

Book/Course	Monday	Tuesday	Wednesday	Thursday	Friday
Language					
Math					
Social Studies					
Science					
Spanish					
English					
Comments					
Teacher Signature					
Tutor/Parent Signature					

required to write down the appropriate page or problem numbers in the correct row.

Announce assignments, and ask students to echo the assignment. Write assignments on the board in a predictable place, color-coded by subject. Or always use one color chalk for homework assignments and a second color for the current in-class assignment. If you use the students' echo to guide you in recording the assignment on the board, you allow students writing time and verify you did indeed announce the assignment.

Ideally, books required for the assignment should be put into the bookbag promptly. Assignments should not be made in the last five minutes of the school day. By that time, half the class has mentally left the classroom.

In the first month of each school year, the teacher or aide should check assignment sheets for accuracy at the end of the day for each student and sign off. Students who demonstrate consistent accuracy can dispense with this service unless they relapse. Students with ADHD are likely to need it throughout the year. In turn, a parent (or tutor) signature should indicate that the homework has been completed and inserted into the To School pocket of the homework folder.

Assignments should be assigned, collected and recorded in an organized fashion that communicates their importance to students. All homework assignments should be collected at the beginning of the day.

Have students get out their homework folders and pass in the work by subject—an easy task if the work is color-coded. Have an aide or monitor promptly check off each sheet to give credit for turning it in (separate from the grade, to be given later). Students whose papers are not turned in can be notified at "materials organization time" of the need to locate the missing papers.

Identify the amount of time that students are expected to work on homework daily, and recommend that they not be allowed to work much longer than that time (to avoid prolonged family homework battles). Use practice problems for homework, so children can do the assignment without parental teaching.

Have frequent specified progress reports for any long-term projects. The first report due may be the student's own proposed outline and schedule for task completion.

Paperwork

Children with ADHD are particularly likely to be disorganized with paperwork. In reading, they can keep track of the line being read with a cardboard or horizontal pencil placed above the line. When writing, using paper that already has "word-blocks" on it or using the finger to space between words helps students with word spacing.

A start symbol at the upper left-hand corner of the page, left to right arrows on the page or a watch or bracelet always on the left (start side) wrist may help the spatially disorganized child. Lefty the Line-Man, a stick figure drawn at the left of each line, facing the letters, is helpful for younger children.

Math worksheets tend to have far too many math problems per page for children with ADHD. If these students try to copy the problems themselves, they are as likely to err in the copying as in the computation, so adult assistance is needed.

Students can more easily keep rows and columns straight if the numbers are written on quarter-inch graph paper. If lined notebook paper is turned sideways, the lines can be used to keep the columns straight.

Word processing is an excellent organizational tool. It should be introduced early to the bright child with ADHD.

Ideas

All of us tend to have some random thoughts, which we harness with more or less effort. The child with ADHD is dealing with more random thoughts and has less ability to organize them. Strategies for organizing ideas will help all students, but they are critical for students with ADHD. As with other organizational strategies, their use should be specifically taught, assigned and rewarded.

Teach brainstorming. All the ideas related to a topic are written down as soon as they come to mind. Then they are categorized. Students can put rectangles around one kind of idea, ovals or triangles around others. Or they can highlight one kind of idea in yellow, others in red or green. Prioritizing the ideas, both within and among categories, leads to an outline with a sequence of letters and numbers.

Mind-mapping is an invaluable visual organizational tool, particularly for that major elementary school literary production, the book report. Students are taught to draw the same "fill in the spaces" design each time they do a book report.

Younger students fill in the spaces with pictures of characters, places and main events, while older students write in the appropriate words. The mind map becomes a visual guide to remembering and organizing the important components of the report.

Formal outlining should be taught once brainstorming and mind-mapping have been well established. Some computer programs, such as PC-Outline by Brown Bag, make the outlining process much easier for students who develop word-processing skills and have access to a computer.

Tasks

Students with ADHD are particularly prone to charging through assignments helter-skelter, hopping around the page, and neglecting to read instructions, note math signs or complete all of the problems.

They should be taught systematic, sequential scanning. This strategy helps students read and decreases the number of skipped problems. It also gives students a reliable tool for looking for the book for the next subject, missing papers and other lost items.

Have students draw a left-to-right scanning line on paperwork to mark their path or write their own sequence numbers as they go. Remember to reward them. Give bonus points when students go through their packs or desks in a systematic, sequential fashion to look for lost objects.

Students with ADHD need very specific instructions written as well as vocalized. If instructions are given orally, students should be required to echo and write them down. Give students credit for underlining the four most important words in the instructions, circling the math signs or rephrasing the instructions.

The steps for a longer assignment need to be stated explicitly and checked for partial credit along the way. Make it clear that the steps, not just the final product, are important. Correct steps lead to a good product.

Similarly, require that all work be shown on math problems. No steps, no credit. (Or give bonus points for showing the work.) Give partial credit if the steps are all correct even if a computation error (common in children with ADHD) results in a wrong answer.

Attention

Attention is the essential first step for learning. Education comes from the word *educare*—to lead oneself out of. Students only receive education if they are actively involved in and attentive to the process.

As mentioned earlier, the challenge to the teacher is to be at once manager, director and actor. The teacher needs to set up the theater so all the seats are comfortable, the sound is good and everyone can see.

Then the teacher writes the script and acts to stimulate the attention and imagination of the students. In this way, students are awakened, drawn in, focused and engaged for the whole affair so they become part of the play.

We have been talking about some of the managing and directing. Now we need to talk about getting the students into the theater and captivated by the drama itself.

Transition

While children with ADHD change tasks all the time, they are not good at changing at the right time. They often seem to get stuck, or perseverate, staying with something too long. Changes also tend to disorganize and lose them.

They need clear, distinguishable signals that change is approaching and that change is occurring. For example, you can flip the lights of the room or the overhead projector off and on as a three-minute warning.

Announce how many minutes are left to work on a project. For younger children, say: "The big hand is on the ten now. When it's on the eleven, it will be time to put away your math." A bell, the word *freeze,* or a clicker may signal the moment for change.

Transitional activities, commonly used by kindergarten teachers, are just as helpful in later grades. Thirty seconds of quiet jogging in place beside the desks can be followed by a quick, eyes-closed, deep-breathing relaxation strategy or a period of quiet stretching between subjects.

One physical education teacher escorted a very energetic group of more than thirty students back to the classroom in absolute silence. They were competing for a pizza party to be given to the class with the most consistent quiet return to their classroom. Music and story reading are restful transitions after lunch or an agitated recess.

Tackle

Tackling, or grabbing the students' attention, is critical. You have to get the lid off before the lessons can begin to pour in the knowledge. Tackling can be aided by such start-now phrases as *focus, ready-set-go, pencils up* or *one, two, three.*

Interesting openers might include asking a mystery question to be answered by the lesson, showing a pertinent cartoon on the overhead, singing a jingle that will be the memory hook for the lesson or doing a brief demonstration. Try to think of a relation between the subject and things you know are interesting to the students (soccer, dinosaurs, birthday parties, bubbles) and start in that context. Since the opener is important, don't start until a hush has fallen over the audience.

When you need to tackle the attention of an individual child, step toward her or him. Rest a hand on her or his desk, a finger on an appropriate spot in her or his book.

Alert the child by stating his or her name, and then ask a question that you know he or she can answer. If you suspect the child is returning from the Land of the Dinosaurs, make the question multiple choice to give a better chance of success, e.g., "John, which is a liquid, oil or salt?"

It's tempting to embarrass such children to make it clear that they should pay better attention. But children are more likely to want to pay attention if they have the right answer. They are more likely to withdraw if they get the answer wrong. The public embarrassment of "wrong again" adds to their low self-esteem burden.

Children with ADHD may intend to pay attention, but the ADHD can make this difficult. Additional negative emotions rather than the learning become the focus, and the child quickly shuts down. Here again, nothing succeeds like success.

Tether

Keeping attention engaged, or tethered, is where the dramatic art of teaching is most enhanced by refined technique. Teaching is an act for the benefit of learning.

Make your teaching audible. Speak using your diaphragm and sinuses, not your throat. Enunciate clearly, using lots of inflection to keep interest level up. When giving directions or instruction to the class, a friendly touch on the shoulder of the student with attentional drift may help her or him stay in tune.

Use a variety of teaching techniques. Learning is both reinforced and more focused if some combination of sight, sound, movement and touch is involved in the same activity. Never rely on a single verbal delivery or transient visual demonstration. If students weren't paying attention at that moment, they will miss it and may lose the thread of the lesson.

Students must always be able to refer back to something. Accompany all verbal presentations with visuals, and use written diagrams or outlines to accompany demonstrations. An overhead projector increases visual attention. (The eye is spontaneously drawn to the light.)

Use colored pasta or straws for math lessons. As you read instructions together, have everyone tie a knot in a piece of yarn for each separate step. Make letters in sand, clay or with big house-painting brushes dipped in water (outside). Music and rhythm are good ways to teach rote material, including math facts, states and capitals, or a foreign language.

Provide lessons on tape to accompany written materials. The earphones at a listening post serve to physically tether the restless child, screen out other sounds, and allow the child to relisten to anything missed. One very energetic kindergarten student with ADHD completed only one formal art project for the year—a big fire engine of rectangles, circles and triangles that he pasted together following instructions the teacher had taped for him.

Computer programs are excellent teaching tools. They use touch and sight (and sometimes hearing), there is minimal waiting time, rewards in accumulated points are given frequently and embarrassment is avoided. Choose programs that start quickly, use only rewards and have adjustable response-speed requirements.

Respect the use of task-related self-talk, or *sub-vocalization,* as a good learning technique. Auditory learners use sub-vocalization to reinforce their learning; children with ADHD use it to keep themselves alert and on-task (better to be talking on the subject than off); and data shows that better learners use it as a learning strategy. Teach students to vocalize quietly rather than asking them to stop vocalizing.

Keep everyone involved all of the time. Time waiting while ten other children take their turns reading or answering questions is almost guaranteed off-task time for a child with ADHD. It's a bit like letting go of the string on a helium balloon. Not directly engaged, the attention of the child with ADHD just drifts away.

Use chorus reading, or quickly shift from child to child word by word or sentence by sentence. Have everyone give simultaneous responses to questions with "one, two or three fingers," answers written on magic slates or chalkboard work.

Ask a question and answer it yourself. Ask it again, and ask the back row to answer. Teach three steps, and then ask the left row to tell you step one, the middle row to tell you step two, and so on. Questions focus the attention. Unison response requests keep all students on their toes.

Keep it lively, and you'll keep the students with you. Unison responses, direct instruction, cooperative learning and peer tutoring can keep all of the students actively engaged.

I watched cross-age tutoring at its best in a large inner-city school. Teachers of a fourth and a first grade class have paired up their students. They bring the students together weekly for a cross-age activity.

I watched the teams create safety posters. The teams demonstrated caring, sharing and respect; intense involvement by every one of the sixty students in the crowded room; and pride in the projects that unfolded. (Children with ADHD typically do much better with children several years older or younger, where the pecking order is clear, than with same-age children.)

Tickle

Tickle the attention of students to help them focus on the most important things. Students with ADHD are notorious for randomly accumulating and remembering bits and pieces of information without a sense of prioritization. Their poor attentional steering seems to leave them without a focus.

In presentations, provide students with outlines of the materials you are going to present, but leave some blanks for them to fill in, perhaps in association with unison response. Check the papers to make sure that each student did fill in the outline correctly, and then return it for students to study. Use different colors to highlight important information, and teach students to do the same.

When giving assignments, tell students how many steps are in the assignment. Then give directions one step at a time, and have the class chorus the response following your cue—first, second, and so on. Give students a list of the specifics to be accomplished during cooperative learning.

The role of attentional fatigue in error patterns, particularly on math worksheets, tends to result in far more errors at the end than at the beginning of a homework or test page. One solution is to divide the work into shorter segments, but students should also be trained to check their work from the bottom up.

On tests, be sure that questions are clear and unequivocal. Use the power of the test as teacher. When you ask students to recall something after studying it once, they will be unable to recall what they didn't initially notice. When given opportunity for a second- chance study, their attention will focus on the areas they had initially missed, giving a much better chance of accuracy.

Therefore, test three times. The first pretest draws attention to the information that will be covered. The second test focuses attention on important details. The third test is the official one. Highlight the value of the second test by letting students keep the higher grade of the second and third tests.

Identify subject matter components that need particular attentional focus. For example: Only symbols change meaning when they change position. A rose, a cup, a dog remain the same from any angle.

When teaching students to write and recognize symbols, use a stick figure at the left of end of each line, with its face looking toward the symbols. Point out that the numbers 1 and 8 face you, but only "silly 6" has its back to the figure. The letter *b* has its back to it, but *d* doesn't.

In reading, have impulsive students draw a line under the second part of the word (the part they usually skip over). Have these students circle or highlight the plus and minus signs before starting to solve a math problem.

Help students focus on the main idea in reading. Introduce a study guide system such as SQ3R (scan, question, read, respond, review) for reading social studies, math and science texts.

- *Scan* the headings, pictures and bold print.
- Read the *questions*.
- *Read* the text, perhaps marking in the margin the number of the question answered by that text.
- *Respond* to the questions.
- *Review.*

In social skills training, focus students' attention on the important aspects of facial expression, body tone and hand action that reflect how a person is feeling.

Transform

Students with ADHD, and some with other special learning challenges, may need modifications to accommodate their individual abilities in addition to general teaching techniques that optimize attention and focus. In a classroom where individualization is the rule rather than the exception, there is little embarrassment at being singled out for special treatment. Tall students need bigger desks, immigrants need language assistance, nearsighted students need reminders to wear their glasses, retarded students need a more elementary curriculum, and ADHD students are special, too.

Be sure that assignment and test expectations are consistent with attentional difficulties and any co-existing learning disabilities. Breaking tasks down into steps makes it easier to adjust the particular step that is difficult for a child.

Have children with printing problems brainstorm, prioritize, outline and narrate their stories. Then it is easier to make some accommodation to the final writing than if the assignment is just to write a story.

Divide worksheets into several shorter portions. Have the child with ADHD get the first portion checked off before going on to the next.

(Permission to go to the teacher's help center with each completed portion may provide a much-needed opportunity for movement.)

Adapt tests to the child's ability to sustain attention. A student with ADHD may do much better on three 15-minute tests than on one 45-minute test. Allow untimed tests for the child with slow memory or writing, and allow an oral test if performance on a written test was poor.

Many inattentive children do poorly on tests because they can't stay focused on the test. These children can do well with the attentional focus provided by a teacher asking the same questions one-on-one. Use multiple choice tests if the student can recognize the right answer but has difficulty with retrieval memory.

Provide a no-fault, low-interruption system for helping the stuck student. The student who doesn't understand the assignment can't get on task. Punishing him or her for being off task does not address the issue.

Dr. Jerry Ammer, a professor of special education, recommends that during seat-work each student have on her or his desk a two-color assistance signal, such as a block that is green on one side and white on the other. When students need assistance, they turn the block over to the green side and get out a folder of practice work meant for such times. The teacher or aide assisting students with seat-work scans for "green side" students, giving assistance as promptly as possible. Such a system avoids restless, waving arms and allows students to continue on a task.

In one teacher's class, a small circle of chairs at a chalkboard by the side of the room acts as "coach's headquarters." After presenting the math lesson and the assignment (with overhead), the teacher steps to the side and invites any students not clear on the lesson or assignment to come to him. Several students come automatically—they always need to have the one-on-one review.

The first student to arrive immediately steps to the board to try to work through the first problem, and each student in turn is coached through a problem at the board. Students get help with no waiting time; they learn from other students and return to their seats as soon as they understand.

The teacher invites anyone whom he notices is off task to join his "team" so he can monitor, encourage and explain. This is discipline, not punishment. It is respectful, educational problem-solving, educational follow-through, the "come here" that nurtures.

A nearby student designated as monitor can provide immediate assistance to surrounding students. Every student in such a help team should have some special contribution. The student with ADHD might be the pencil sharpener—another respectful way to give "legal motion."

Arrange for one-on-one tutoring, daily if necessary, to fill in the gaps where the attention was wandering. (Some schools provide tutoring as part of a low-cost after-school childcare program.)

Special involvement in the lesson presentation may keep the attention focused. Involve students with ADHD in demonstrations—writing on the board, holding supplies, demonstrating how to head the paper, and so on. Use your seating arrangements to make this easier.

Find out if students are more or less attentive when fidgeting with something or when listening to music. Some (but not most) students with ADHD are much more attentive to discussions when building with Legos or playing with a mechanical pencil than when they just have to communicate.

Some visual learners do best if they are required to draw a diagram of the topic being discussed. A few students read better to music. (Don't go just on report; test it out.)

Accommodate the tendency to lose track of things. Families may be well advised to get an extra supply of textbooks and keep one set at home. Then the books are available for homework, and the child can mark related comments, underline the most important words, and so on.

Have extra supplies for the "Leaky Loser" who is never paying attention when she or he puts something down. Develop a private reward system for keeping track of equipment and belongings, but don't nag the child about it.

Dealing with Other Difficulties

The speed spurts and steering errors of the child with ADHD tend to create a variety of special challenges that can benefit from special attention. Again, most of these intervention strategies can be done with the entire classroom.

Momentum

Children with ADHD need assistance with pacing and self-monitoring. They tend either to drift off task or to go much too quickly. The comment "If you'd only slow down!" reflects the problem but doesn't help the student whose brakes are stuck.

Divide work time into small units (five to fifteen minutes) with a timer or description of movement of the hands on the clock. ("You'll be starting on this when the big hand is on three and finished when it is on five. That's ten minutes.") Clarify that the assignment is to be completed within that time period. That keeps the focus.

To decrease rushing, clarify that getting done early means more time for careful checking, not time to do anything else. Clearly define the level of acceptable accuracy and thoroughness.

Students who are capable of better work but tend to just put down any answer to get the assignment done need clear performance guidelines before they begin. Specify five sentences of at least five words each rather than just requesting a paragraph. Specify a bonus point for each correct punctuation mark rather than just marking all the errors afterward.

Movement

For many children with ADHD, the need to move seems like the need to cough—it's very difficult to suppress. Remember that a medication level that completely suppresses the hyperactivity may be too high for clear thinking. Legitimate opportunities for movement allow the child to get on with the process of learning.

Frequent whole-class exercise breaks, particularly at transition times as described earlier, benefit everyone. All the students stand on signal, run or jump at the side of the desk for a brief count, and then sit down. Order is maintained by clarifying and enforcing strict silence and no-nonsense rules to permit prompt return to focus.

Individualized in-class movement options include the previously discussed pencil-sharpener duty and divided worksheets, as well as permission to stand or kneel at the desk as long as the student is quiet and does not lose touch with the desk.

If a child is allowed to do errands that include exercise, you may need to require the child's return within a designated time period to keep the privilege. Very restless children who have difficulty remembering to get back to the classroom may benefit from the Post-It race described in the section on Protection from Embarrassment in Chapter 4.

To help young children stay seated at circle time, spread a large bean-bag snake across their laps as an anchor. (Invite everyone to have such a snake, but make sure the very wiggly child always has one if it helps.) Individualized contract rewards for limited sitting time may help these children survive circle time.

In higher grades, all students may be invited to choose to turn their chairs around so that they sit straddling the chair, leaning over the chair back. This position encourages staying seated because it is more difficult to get up. It also provides stabilizing support for the chest, helpful to those children who have some difficulty just holding their bodies still.

Golden silence bonus points may assist students to refrain from talking at the wrong time and blurting out answers without permission.

Avoid using recess and lunch hours for remedial work. Encourage playground activities and walking to school before the beginning of the school day.

Moods

Problems in controlling emotions can be disruptive to the classroom and embarrassing to the student who "loses it." Timely intervention requires vigilance to see storms coming rather than waiting for the full eruption.

If students have already received classroom training in relaxation strategies, the teacher can have the whole class take a minute or two to "float on a cloud" when several students appear to be getting out of control. Class jogging, stretching, soothing music or a one-minute reading from a joke book may avert the storm.

The teacher may develop a code word with the individual moody student—a supportive "I need you" that gives the student permission to go to a designated protected place such as the counselor's office or the rest table in a neighboring classroom. Embarrassment and failure are likely to cause emotional outbursts.

Try to be protective, supportive and enabling. Children with ADHD may be moody and depressed throughout the school year because of their incompatibility with the classroom requirements, yet be able to enjoy being out of school.

Communicate carefully with parents regarding mood difficulties. Be sure to note the time, since rebound moodiness may be a sign that medication is wearing off too soon. A gradual escalation in moodiness may be a sign of medication's side effects, deepening depression, or escalating peer or extracurricular stresses that need professional assistance.

Memory

An extensive review of learning strategies is beyond the scope of this book, but memory inconsistency is so common in children with ADHD that some attention to memory issues is warranted. Children with ADHD have difficulty selectively storing memories, because they do not sustain the attentional focus to notice and process the appropriate data unless they find the subject intriguing.

They may have difficulty getting memories out of storage because they are too impulsive to systematically reflect, or check the memory files, before giving a response. They need cognitive-behavioral training in memory storage and retrieval.

There are several basics regarding memory.

- It is easier to retrieve one big memory "chunk" (the alphabet song) than a lot of little separate pieces (26 letters). Songs, rhymes, raps, stories and pictures make good chunks. (That's why Esteem Kid and Y-Man are included in this book.)

- New information that can be linked to existing knowledge is easier to remember. ("Baa, Baa, Black Sheep" and "Twinkle, Twinkle, Little Star" are the same tune as the alphabet song).

- People vary regarding the relative strength of their seeing, listening and movement/touch memories, but everyone remembers better if all three (multimodality techniques) are used at the same time.

- Errors are just as likely to be remembered as non-errors. Practice information correctly rather than trying to guess before studying. (Don't use flash cards or other systems that encourage guessing to teach new information.)

- Study, Test, Check, Restudy, Retest, Recheck gives practice in memory retrieval as well as multimodality memory storage. For instance, in rehearsing new math facts, such as $7 + 5 = 12$:

  - Study—read, write and say the fact.

  - Test—cover it up. Can you write and say it?

  - Check—look at the problem again.

  - Restudy—again read, write and say it.

  - Retest—cover it again. Write and say it again. (Note, this is the fourth time doing it correctly.)

  - Recheck—check again. Say it.

- Six accurate rehearsals of the same information, with reinforcement within an eight-hour period, move one a long leap toward permanent memory. In the previous example, five rehearsals were done, probably four accurately. Another round of Study, Test, Check will move those facts into permanent memory territory.

- We remember best information that interests us or feels important to us. Start by asking an important question, which draws attention to the interest or importance of the information to be taught.

- Immediate listening memory (which lets you repeat back a number or name as soon as you hear it) is temporary in everyone—just a few seconds. Immediate visual memory lasts almost no time. To convert these to stored memory, teach the students to:

  - Immediately use see-say for visual information—translate things they see into words they can say.

  - Revocalize the information every two seconds to keep the immediate listening memory alive.

  - Elaborate—chunk, link, make a visual image if the information was received in words.

  - Rehearse—say it over several (six) times.

  - Reinforce—go back over the information several hours later.

As you prepare lessons, try to find picture summaries of verbal information, links to things known and important to the students, and multimodality techniques to keep all students actively participating in learning with all their learning channels. Consider leaving the last half hour of each day for review of all new information and clarification of homework.

Magnificence

Remember Esteem Kid and the four components of self-esteem—a sense of being in control (head), a sense of competence (muscles), a sense of being valued (heart) and protection from embarrassment (clothing). These components are important for every student.

For each struggling child in your class, list several areas of excellence. Think about how to build on those areas. For example, invite the verbal child to give oral reports, do a bit of official stand-up comedy or participate in readers' theater.

One fourth grader with ADHD had a writing difficulty that resulted in ultra-short book reports. This student was invited to tape an imaginary interview with several of the characters for his next report.

His divergent excellence and verbal skills resulted in a magnificent success. The student was rewarded with the appreciative laughter and applause of his classmates, a high grade for the records and a big boost both in his self-esteem and his interest in the next book.

Post the airplane drawings or stick-figure extravaganzas of the budding artists; have a "Legos fair" for the chronic Legos builders; and invite students to bring favorite dinosaurs, baseball cards or homemade creations for sharing.

Encourage children with ADHD to participate in walking, biking, swimming, and aikido or other martial arts. (Students with ADHD are generally better in activities where they are constantly involved with no waiting. Baseball should be reserved only for students with ADHD who demonstrate great talent in the game.) Offer a track and field meet as a class reward for bonus points, and have a ribbon for the "movingest" kid.

Avoid restricting participation in the child's areas of strength due to problems in other areas. Draw attention to the strengths. Post a picture of each child doing something well on her or his desk. Point out to the parents the child's strengths. They'll thank you forever.

Membership

Students with ADHD, particularly those who are oppositional or have associated learning difficulties, are easily excluded socially. They may tend to alienate themselves through bossy or aggressive behavior. They tend to be better at making friends than keeping them.

Social skills training, discussed earlier, is very beneficial. Rehearse way-out-of-trouble phrases in class roleplays:

- No problem!
- My pleasure!
- That was a mistake (I made). I'm sorry.
- Everyone makes mistakes sometimes. It's OK.
- Which do you prefer?
- Here, you go first.
- Thanks for noticing (in response to teasing).

Do class pantomimes of different emotions—half the class acts them out while the other half tries to guess what they are.

Encourage cross-age playmates, pairing students who are two or three years apart. Group activities such as singing, where each student is too busy doing his or her own thing to worry what anyone else is doing, are helpful. Assign a socially struggling student to a special helper role (cleaning the chalkboards), and invite her or him to choose a different helper each day.

One teacher, in response to some classroom discord, instituted Friendship Day several times a month. Each child brought or prepared in class a gift for a mystery friend whose name he or she had drawn.

Students prepared a decorated lunch bag, a note of praise or appreciation, a public tribute or special song for the mystery friend. Sharing a pencil, holding the door and other acts of kindness for the friend for the day were also encouraged.

With each Friendship Day, the children learned from each other more ways to show friendship. They thought about what was special about a student with whom they might otherwise have had little contact. They also felt the warmth of being treated as a special friend themselves. The classroom discord vanished, and a very cohesive, caring spirit took its place.

Medication

The teacher is usually presented with one of two situations regarding medication. First, what do you need to do if a child in your room is already on stimulant medication? Second, what do you do if you think medication might benefit a child who is in your classroom?

If a child in your classroom is on medication you should take the following steps:

- ❧ Speak with the school health staff (or parents) to clarify the medication, dose and time that the medication is to be taken.

- ❧ Make every effort to see that the student gets to the office at the correct time for a school dose.

- ❧ Maintain absolute respect for the child's right to privacy with regard to the medication.

- ❧ Provide the parents and prescribing physician with your observations regarding performance and behaviors that may be related to medication benefits or side effects.

- ❧ Read over the information in Chapter 3 and Appendix F regarding medication, with particular attention to the medication the child is using.

If you feel that medication for ADHD may benefit a student in your room, it is definitely time to share the load. Speak with the parents and the school nurse about the difficulties you are seeing, but do not try to diagnose or prescribe. Remember, not all inattentive, impulsive, hyperactive children have ADHD. It may be very appropriate to recommend having a bike specialist check to see if anything can help the child whose bike keeps going off the path. It is inappropriate, however, to recommend a particular set of pliers.

Share the Load

As a teacher, you play a tremendous role in the lives of your students. The follow-up studies of Weiss and Hechtman (1987, p. 295-296) documented that it was often a teacher or other school staff member who made all the difference in the life of a child growing up with ADHD. You can embark on the ROADS strategies of this chapter to the benefit of all your students without knowing the diagnosis of any child.

But the struggling child does need further help—and you deserve help, too. As discussed earlier, careful diagnosis is important to identify if the inattentive, impulsive child really has neurologically based ADHD. It is equally important to identify what other factors may contribute to the student's difficulties. Many factors can cause similar symptoms that should be treated in other ways.

The school team, the parents and outside professionals, including the child's physician, all have roles to play in understanding and aiding the child with attention and impulse control difficulties. Each of these children should be reviewed by the school study team or its equivalent.

Every effort should be made to establish and maintain supportive communication with the family, with respect for the challenges they are probably facing at home. Invite the parents to sit in the classroom to observe. Do not insist that the child has ADHD or that he or she be taken to see a specialist. Do encourage parents to see, and let you share information with, their own physician.

There are many areas in which family and other professional assistance may be merited:

- Sleep and diet
- Health problems, including poor vision and hearing
- Atari or Nintendo excess or too much television
- Relatives' stresses and family needs
- Embarrassment in front of relatives and peers

- Learning disabilities
- Organizational problems of the child's environment at school and home
- Anxiety
- Depression
- Strategies, training and needs that require the skill of outside professionals

The school nurse can help coordinate with the teacher, the parents and the physician to address most of the SHARE issues, as well as medication, if that is involved. The psychologist, resource specialist, guidance and administrative staff will be involved with the LOADS issues, along with outside educational and mental health providers when needed. The information in Chapter 2 and Appendix C may assist these professionals.

Chapter 7

The Home Front

On a bike trip the family of the boy whose bike has poor steering and brakes may need to work harder to enjoy the outing and avoid yelling. However, this family could choose to do an activity that won't involve the bike, while the family of a child with ADHD may be reminded of the child's attention and impulse control difficulties throughout the day, year after year. This family's challenge is to provide both the necessary "rubber walls" for a safe trip and to provide the child with the nurturing and encouragement critical to self-esteem.

Helping the child feel his or her best is a first priority. In addition to providing for adequate sleep and food, parents should consider the various factors discussed under Share the Load at the end of Chapter 6 and the discussion in Appendix B.

Family problems and tensions are disturbing to any child, but particularly so to children who have unusual difficulty understanding their own feelings as well as those of others. Do not become so focused on your child's internal challenges that you neglect to address problems facing the people she or he loves and needs.

Earlier chapters in this book offer a foundation in adaptations, behavior management strategies, cognitive-behavioral training, drug therapy, issues of esteem and feelings, and action planning. In this chapter we will review some basics of behavioral management in the home and look at a variety of common home challenges, including difficult times of the day, family dynamics, school-related issues, childcare and recreation.

Behavior Management Strategies at Home

Parents have a responsibility to establish guidelines as well as provide opportunities. It can take a great deal of work and energy to provide well for a child, particularly if the child is long on complaint and short on cooperation. There are some strategies, however, which can make the job easier.

Rules and Schedules

Lack of environmental organization at home or school can be troubling, as can a lack of clarity about rules and expectations. The following guidelines can be helpful.

- Have pictures or lists of important rules.
- Choose only rules that are worth enforcing, and enforce these thoroughly.
- Enforce rules with immediate follow-through and logical consequences.
- Don't discuss rules until the child is paying attention.
- Post schedules of daily routines.
- Set a timer for each daily task.

Running a house with rules is not unlike coaching a team, except that parents create, as well as enforce, the rules of the game. Start with a coordinated coaching crew to help the child's team win. Good relationships between coaches and team members are essential, but the coaches should hold the line on appropriate and inappropriate ways to play the game.

All adults involved in caring for a child in the home must agree on their major priorities. They must also reach some general agreement about how rules will be enforced.

Start by drawing up three lists. The first should list everything that bothers you about the child's behavior. List everything you like about what the child does in a second. List things that give the child pleasure in the third.

Each adult then ranks the things that he or she feels are the three most important negative behaviors to discourage and the three most important positive behaviors to encourage. The list of the child's pleasures is the reference for rewards. The highest ranking items are the places to start. Don't sweat the small stuff.

When trying to decide if something is a rule or a recommendation, ask if the child will run into an "electric fence"—a harsh life consequence— if that rule were broken. If so, make it a rule and build a rubber wall to keep the child away from the electric fence of life. For example, a car becomes the potential "electric shock" to the child who runs out into the street. "Stop, look and listen before crossing" is an important rule which merits establishing rubber walls.

Discuss each rule with the child, and ask the child to explain the rule back to you or to another child. It may be helpful to involve the child in thinking of consequences for infractions and compliance.

Remember to couch rules positively:

- We need more room for warm fuzzies around here, so we'll have to figure out how to get rid of the cold pricklies.

- We love you too much to let you ——.

- That's my I-love-you policy.

You may need to change posted household rules. The basic issues may not change, but some rules get followed so automatically that they no longer need posting, while new developmental stages may bring new challenges.

Rules need to be reviewed regularly. Even if the rules stay the same, change the consequences frequently. Children with ADHD respond best to novelty, variety and brevity.

Because much of the management of a busy household revolves around timing to meet everyone's needs and responsibilities, schedule guidelines are best developed at the same time as rules.

Going to the Mat

In making any set of rules, ask yourself: "Would I be willing to 'go to the mat' for this one?" If not, you're talking about a recommendation, not a rule.

What does it mean to go to the mat? It means taking charge and going all the way, being decisive and following through. The tools for going to the mat include Y-Man. Get the child's attention, lay the communication foundation, allow discussion, and then pronounce the decision.

In the case of taking medication, the decision is made in the physician's office, which is where much of the discussion should take place. Once the decision is made, there is the clear "stuck-record" restatement of the decision—the medication must be taken until the next contact with the doctor.

The child may wish to write or tape-record his or her feelings about the medication so they can be conveyed to the physician. The child can do this after the medication is taken, and you may offer to facilitate communication with the physician. But, nevertheless, the day's dose must be taken.

Behind the decisive words stands the follow-through. Usually, all that is required is the parent's presence; do not leave the child's side until the medication is taken. No television, no friends, no progression toward the day until it is down.

You may feel that you can't win, that the child can outwait you. If you do feel that way, the child almost certainly knows it, and will win the battle. Realize that you *can* outwait the child. (The child is, after all, more impatient than you.) As Mark Twain says, "If a man thinks he can or thinks he can't, he is probably right." Think you can, and you will.

With a very determined child, this waiting routine could cause havoc in the morning. But to let the child determine the outcome in such a circumstance (or in any situation where it is worth going to the mat) confuses the issue of who's in charge and grants a disconcerting degree of power to the child. It also begins the process of intermittent reinforcement of negative behavior, as described in the example of the candy machine in Chapter 3.

The line is clear and unchanging—the medicine must go down. Y-Man helps hold the line: Acknowledge the child's concerns; look respectfully at feelings; make adaptations such as giving privacy or finding a medicine with a better taste. Use a behavioral system, together with effective communication and decisive follow-through.

Some Logical Consequences

Logical consequences, which can be used long-term, include the following:

- Time out for impulsive misbehavior—one minute per year of age.

- For fights, send both children to different rooms for time out or send a playmate home.

- Immediate loss of a misused object (time out for the toy).

- Bag toys that are repeated causes of difficulty, either because of fights over them, misuse or abuse, or because they're not put away. (Children with ADHD usually do better with fewer things anyway.)

- For rudeness, use a response cost with loss of a token or penny. Start the day with a number of pennies. (Be guided by how much trouble the child is having. You need enough to last the day.) Each time the child is rude, remove one penny. (This reflects the idea that each day you get 24 hours full of possibilities for joy, which you diminish each time you are unkind to others).

- Catch children being good. Designate a "best behavior" time. For that half hour, reward each five minutes that children are good (with a star, happy face, etc.). When they have enough credits, they can have a special treat (such as watching Mom or Dad turn a somersault, being read a story, etc.).

- Team power—when several children are together, reward them only when everyone is getting along well.

Remember that you *can* establish a set of household rules; it does make a difference; and it's a lot easier than screaming. You might want to figure out a way to reward the family adults (yourself, if you do it alone) for getting together once a month to look over the routines and challenges.

Daily Challenges

Certain tasks and times of the day can be particularly challenging for children with ADHD and their parents. Let's look at some of the turns along the day's path where "crashes" frequently occur.

Awakening

Some people wake up cheerfully. Some have a very difficult time waking up. The person responsible for waking another is viewed as a very unwelcome intruder into the private peace of sleep. The awakener may be greeted with anything from a simple frown to verbal insults and flailing arms.

In the child with ADHD, the course of the day often seems to be determined by the first few minutes. Some children seem to get stuck for the day in the mood of those first minutes, so the awakening can be crucial.

How's the child feeling? Sleepy, and perhaps reluctant to face another day of the frustration of school. How are you feeling? Sleepy, and rushed to get through all the morning's "gotta-do's." If waking up at 7:30 is a problem on school days, but the child is up by 6:30 on the weekends, you can be pretty sure that school isn't agreeing with him or her.

If the problem occurs only when you wake the child and never when your spouse does, give your spouse the pleasure—or find out if there is some special trick you could use for the days when you have wake-up duty. You may need to schedule an extra fifteen minutes every morning for yourself so that you aren't feeling so rushed. Such "front-end alignment" can help the steering for the rest of the day.

Try to separate the waking duty from the person. This can be accomplished easily if the child can be awakened with an alarm or clock radio, a mechanical rouser. The child must be helped to take ownership of getting up. He or she may do well with a contract that gives a reward for setting the alarm (one credit) and another for getting up with the alarm (second credit).

Teddy Bear Tickles lets a favorite stuffed animal do the job. A puppet could also work. Mom or Dad sits on the edge of the bed, stuffed friend in hand. No words are spoken. The stuffed animal may start giving the child a gentle backrub, doing some somersaults on the back. The animal can go on a sniffing tour of the neck and ears, a peek over the top of the head, and a cozy cuddle into the tummy.

Some children with ADHD are very uncomfortable with certain kinds of touch, so watch for those touches that bring something other than the hoped-for smile. The parent's silence is important. The child must be the first one to speak.

Smothered with Smooches might occur instead of or right after Teddy Bear Tickles. A colleague of mine found this the best way to start the day off right with her vivacious son. She would tell him, "I have to get all of these kisses in now because there won't be time later." For this macho eight year old, public kisses from Mom were unacceptable, but in the privacy of bed, the multiple kisses resulted in a smile that would grow until it spread into a big grin across his face. The day would be ready to begin, right side up.

Clothing Conundrums

Clothing conundrums are a common problem of childhood, which may be more pronounced in a child with ADHD. Such a child is likely to be "tactilely defensive." These children are unable to screen out distracting and annoying touch sensations, including scratchy clothing. They tend to be chronically unsatisfied and insatiable, always distracted by what they don't have, aren't doing, or aren't wearing. The oppositional child may have an intense desire for autonomy and control. The results:

- Decisions may be difficult.
- The child may refuse to wear anything but the softest, oldest clothes, with the labels removed and the holes left unmended.
- Whatever you choose may be wrong.
- Over the course of the day, five sets of clean clothes may be scattered about the bedroom.

What is the child feeling? She or he probably feels truly uncomfortable in new jeans and springy elastic, due to the tactile defensiveness. He or she may be convinced that a particular look or feel is right in the eyes of peers.

The child may desperately want to be in charge in some arena of life. He or she may be driven by the healthy growth-force in each of us that moves us toward independence.

What are you feeling? You certainly feel irritated by the thought of the brand new clothes waiting in the drawer (or on the floor where they were thrown in the hunt for "comfy clothes"). You may feel that the holes in your child's old clothes reflect badly on you. You're also irritated by the instant havoc wreaked on those clothes you'd put away so neatly.

It's time for some sorting and prioritization. The child's feelings are valid (they are real), and so are yours. The questions are, What feelings can be helped, and, What are the absolutes in the world of clothing? Safety is usually not an issue here. The economics of laundry water and unused new clothes may be a valid issue. How can you arrive at a win-win solution?

First, when buying clothes, choose what the child will feel comfortable in, not what is featured in the fashion pages. Consider getting hand-me-down or secondhand clothes for children who like the clothes softened up. Be sure to launder new clothes before their first wearing, so they don't get put in the too-stiff category.

If your child only likes black sweatpants, just get lots of black sweatpants (and knee patches with which to mend them). Having several of the same items of clothing makes decisions easier and decreases changes of clothes.

Decide which days and events are really critical regarding clothing, and let children choose the rest of the time. On critical days, give them two or three options to choose from, so they still have autonomy. A selection of three or four capes or aprons (squares of different colored fabric with cloth ties) may satisfy the urge to change clothing.

Above all, if a clothing decision is not an absolute, if you're not willing to go to the mat for it, don't even mention it. Absolutes include covering private parts and protecting feet from cuts and blisters. For me (and most schools), not advertising alcoholic beverages is an absolute. Obviously, a school uniform becomes an absolute, but you may be able to find comfortable variants on the official dress. As for the clothes all over the floor, let's think about that when we discuss cleaning the room.

Medication Management

If medication is used, timing is important. It needs to coincide with school schedules, as well as the availability of morning adult supervision. Because the medication will cause loss of appetite, the child needs to eat breakfast within the first half hour of taking it. (While medication is not absorbed quite as well when taken with food as it is on an empty stomach, the difference is not great enough to justify missing breakfast [Swanson et al., 1983]).

The actual schedule needs to be worked out with the physician, so that the school medication permission form reflects the appropriate time for school doses. Make an effort to have the school dose timing coincide with normal school transitions for recess or lunch.

In some households, the difficulty of mornings makes it worthwhile to give the child the medication, perhaps with milk or another protein-rich beverage, as soon as she or he awakens. Then the child can be left alone until the medication has had a chance to get her or his steering ready for the day. An adult must be available to supervise the taking of the medication.

One hazard of giving medication to inattentive children is that they may not remember if they have taken it. Thus, if one parent has already given the dose, leaves, and the other parent wasn't told, a second dose may be given inadvertently. To prevent this, the medication can be put into a seven-day pill dispenser, kept in a safe place out of reach of small fingers. Then it's immediately clear if the dose has been given.

What if a child decides he or she doesn't want to take the medicine? Here one arrives at the mat. If you and the physician have agreed that the prescribed medication is beneficial and important to your child's well-being, taking the medicine is not optional.

On the other hand, the child's feelings about the medication are very important. Let the child know that he or she may speak with the physician about his or her feelings.

Feeling different or embarrassed or not feeling good on the medication are legitimate issues. They merit physician consultation, no matter how well behaved the child may be on the current schedule. But a change in medication cannot occur until the child and you have spoken with the doctor and received new orders.

It would be very appropriate, at some other time of the day, to do some team problem solving with the child: "I worry that you feel uncomfortable about taking the medicine, but I'd be sad to see you having problems at school just because your steering and brakes were out of whack. I get upset, too, because we have so much to do in the morning, but we end up getting mad at each other over that little tiny pill. If we can figure out what bothers you about it, maybe we can solve that problem and still let you have your steering work for you."

If the medication tastes bitter, perhaps a spoonful of honey, yogurt or jelly would help for now. A brand-name prescription might be better the next time (generics tend to spend less money on the niceties of taste).

Maybe a reward would help, offering bonus points for taking the medication without complaint. Perhaps the child would be more comfortable if you brought the medication privately to the bedroom where teasing siblings wouldn't upset her or him.

Breakfast Choices

A good breakfast is important for three reasons. First, because your grandmother said so, and grandmothers are usually right. Second, because it needs to last until lunch, or at least until mid-morning snack when children are at school. And third, data indicate that protein-containing foods taken early in the day benefit attentional focus.

This benefit is probably due to the role of tyrosine, an amino acid that comes from protein. It is the chemical from which the catecholamines, dopamine and norepinephrine, are made. Choices include:

- peanut butter on toast
- cream cheese on a bagel
- left-over pizza, chicken or roast beef
- melted cheese on a tortilla
- a piece of string cheese
- a carton of yogurt
- a powdered instant breakfast mixed with milk
- some lunch meat
- a glass of milk

Another advantage of protein over carbohydrates like bread and cereal is that it takes longer to digest, so one doesn't feel hungry as quickly after a glass of milk as after two pieces of toast.

A Morning Schedule

Mornings tend to be stressful in most households, as everyone has different places to be within a fairly short period of time. Morning conflicts can upset the entire day, so they are particularly important to avoid. Be sure to allow yourself enough time. Help the child think through and develop a personal schedule using cognitive tools.

Have the child tell you all the things she or he has to do in the morning and how much time she or he thinks is needed to get them all done. You might ask if any of these things are difficult to do and if the child could do any of them more cheerfully the night before.

Write the morning activities down, or draw picture symbols if the child doesn't yet read. Then have the child tell you what else he or she would like to be able to do in the morning before school and the time school (or another "official" place) starts.

Show the child the amount of time available. Have the child help you fit the tasks into place on a clock or timeline for the morning.

You might make a Morning Routines poster using photographs of the child putting on clothes, brushing teeth, eating breakfast, and collecting school books and lunch. Now see if there is any time left for the child's choice of activity (assuming it is something he or she would have permission to do).

Give the child a timer to keep track of the time planned for each task. Reward her or him for completion of each step (cluster tasks into five- to fifteen-minute units). As a child succeeds with the individual steps, she or he can be rewarded for completing the entire morning routine in a timely fashion by getting to enjoy the remaining time at the preferred activity.

Bedding Down

At the end of the day, bedtime routines need to be predictable, secure and relaxing. Children with ADHD may have unusual difficulty both falling asleep and staying asleep, although they sleep extremely deeply at other times. (Bed-wetting into elementary school years is common in children with ADHD.) Inadequate sleep intensifies problems of restlessness, inattention and poor mood control.

While "winding-up" silliness is sometimes a joyful part of early evening activity, children with ADHD need a calm transition into sleep. For children who have difficulty getting to sleep, an hour is not too much time for bathing and brushing, being read to, lights out, and backrubs and quiet conversation in bed.

In homes with a child with ADHD, this time can be particularly special. No one is more willing to listen to a story, a song or poem, a tale of what was good about the day or statements of philosophy and faith than a child who doesn't want to let the day end.

Tuck-in time may be the only time that hyperactive children hold still long enough to receive a hug or a rub and to hear the gentle encouraging words you want to say to them. Start tuck-in early enough to enjoy it without running into sleep time.

The schedule dictates an end even to this special time, and the end needs to be honored consistently to allow the child good rest. At the designated time, a favorite rhyme, song, prayer or saying marks the day's close, and the parent leaves the room.

There is no turning back for the parent, and no coming out for the child. Siblings who share a room must maintain silence. There is no radio, television or tape recorder. The child may whisper in the dark to a stuffed animal or doll.

For the child who has significant difficulties getting to sleep, the weekend sleep schedule should vary little more than a half-hour from the weekday schedule. A child who is up late Friday and Saturday nights has difficulty getting back to sleep at a reasonable time on Sunday. Then he or she ends up with Monday morning jet-lag.

It is much easier to stay up a little later for several nights than to fall asleep earlier. School and other day schedules can't be moved later to accommodate later and later bedtimes, so bedtime consistency is necessary.

Be cautious about taking the child out with you for after-dinner shopping or evening events. Team with other parents to have consistent, reasonable, enforced bedtimes when a child spends the night with a friend.

Cleaning the Room

Go clean your room. The order sounds so easy, but in fact it's a difficult chore. Cleaning the room is a highly distracting task. Each toy the child touches invites him or her to play with it. The disorganization of the room blurs all the directional signs that might tell the child which way to go first. Techniques are definitely needed, and simplicity is of the essence.

The first step is to avoid purchasing too many belongings. Children with

ADHD prefer to run around outside much of the time anyway, despite their wails for every single action figure. Consider dividing toys into two groups and rotating them. Then children have fewer toys to deal with at one time, and they can enjoy the novelty of toys they haven't seen for a while.

Brown Bag Booty offers a natural consequence way to make this happen. Toys that aren't put away within an appropriate time frame are taken as "pirate's booty" in a brown bag. They are kept out of circulation for a period of time and reintroduced later.

Trading Post Rules are a second approach to easing the clean-up and minimizing the clutter. Sort the toys (and capes) into several baskets, grouping things that are used together. Store all the baskets in a closed cabinet out of the child's room that is off-limits.

The child is allowed to have only one basket at a time. Before he or she can get another basket, the child must toss all of the first set of toys into the first basket and return it to the trading post.

A clothing check needs to be made at regular intervals, depending on the frequency of clothing changes. Dropping dirty clothes in the hamper is an appropriate morning chore. Be sure the hamper has an open top—the extra step of opening the hamper may be too much for the impulsive child.

If the child changes clothes frequently, you may want to have a drawer set aside for nearly clean clothes, and check on clothes at each trading post exchange or at meal times. Hanging clothes up on hangers is very difficult for impulsive children; it may require considerable adult follow-through.

Family Matters

Some challenges involve the entire family. Meals, relationships with sisters and brothers, chores, separate households and childcare are areas deserving special consideration.

Dinnertime Debates

A sit-down dinner may be difficult for a young child, particularly if that child has ADHD. The desired family togetherness deteriorates into chaos. Conflict arises over staying seated, eating rather than playing with food, the use of metal utensils, and other issues of manners.

When it comes to eating, children with the hyperactivity of ADHD are born nomads, meant to eat on the run. If parents feel strong enough about a sit-down family meal time to go to the mat for it, they may need to develop an action plan for success.

Generally, it is advisable to adapt. Bring the family together for several minutes around the table, but reserve more sustained family time for later fun, reading and relaxing. If children can't leave their parents in peace to eat but won't eat with them, dinnertime may be an appropriate time for authorized video or television viewing.

Children are likely to do better snacking on peanut butter sandwiches and carrot sticks than wailing over their reluctant adventures with baked chicken and beans. As they mature, you can lengthen the "sit-together" time.

Provide guidance for nutritional food selection despite flexible timing and menu. Junk foods (high in calories, low in vitamins, minerals and proteins) interfere with a child's normal tendency to eat a nutritionally balanced diet.

Sibling Squabbles

Team Time or Happy Hour may decrease sibling squabbles. During these designated times, group rewards are earned if everyone is cooperating or simply if no one is arguing or fighting. Accumulate pennies, beans or popcorn in a jar (not a good idea in the presence of small children who might choke on them) or stars or marks on a chart.

When the target is achieved, there is a family event—a pizza party, time to bake cookies, an appropriate video or movie. *Siblings Without Rivalry* by Adele Faber and Elaine Mazlish (Hearst Books, 1987) is an excellent resource on the issue of sibling relationships.

When one or more children in a family have ADHD, adults may need to intervene to protect the siblings from each other and to help the children better understand each other's strengths and challenges. The brothers and sisters of children with ADHD may resent both the immediate annoyances of the impulsivity and the drain on parental resources. These children, too, need some time alone with the parents. Family counseling may be very beneficial.

Chores

Chores are a part of family living and a precursor of larger life responsibilities. Adapt chores to the individual child. Setting the table is an excellent task for teaching and reinforcing right/left orientation. For the young child who is unsure, laminate placemats with a picture of a fork and the word LEFT and a picture of a knife and spoon and the word RIGHT in appropriate places.

Children with ADHD may enjoy washing dishes, but the experience may be more relaxing for all if that chore is reserved for times when non-breakable table settings are used. Group family projects, whether window washing or gardening, can be excellent opportunities for the parents to model both organization and positive attitudes toward work.

Two-Household Considerations

With our society's high rate of separation and divorce, many children have two homes. For the child with ADHD, the need for predictability and consistency needs special consideration in such situations.

However, the expectation for identical rules between houses is impractical; different parenting styles probably were part of the reason for separation in the first place. Children can adapt to different rules in different places as long as there is consistency within each household.

It is much easier for children if they have the same schedule each weekday that involves homework, usually Monday through Thursday. Four types of schedules allow this. In some families, the children are based in one household and visit the other on some or all of the weekends. In others, vacations (and perhaps some weekends) are in one home and school weeks are spent in the other.

Where more equal custody arrangements are desired, the children may spend Monday evening through Friday morning in one home, but go directly to and from the "weekend" home on Friday afternoon and Monday mornings. A fourth schedule, which works if one of the parents is available after school, is for the students to go to the same home each day, Monday through Friday, after school, and be picked up by the other parent for evenings.

This schedule offers time with each parent on a daily basis. A clear schedule is arranged for homework to be done (usually with the afternoon parent who maintains communication with the school), and weekends can be alternated. For any child, adequate sleeping arrangements, which do not include the child sleeping in the parent's bed, are very important.

Who's Watching the Kids?

After-school supervision is a significant issue for children with ADHD if a parent is not available. Large childcare programs that are loosely supervised and minimally structured provide inadequate protection from the social disruptions that result from impulsivity.

Ideally, an after-school childcare setting for school-age children with ADHD should provide the following:

- Homework supervision. (By the time working parents get home, medication has worn off, everyone is too tired, and the important nurturing role of the family needs to take priority.)

- Nutritious snacks, which do not include foods to which children are sensitive. (When medication wears off, the child is often very hungry.)

- Play time supervised by a mature, attentive individual who can both aid the children in social skills development and intervene in a timely fashion when difficulties arise. (Sports such as soccer, in which everyone plays, are excellent.)

- Predictable rules and schedules. (Good behavioral management is important wherever the child is.)

- A quiet place for those who prefer to curl up with some comic books, a card game, etc.

- Safety. (Impulsive children do not stop to think before they act.)

- Compatible children. (Age distribution of playmates should include someone with whom developmental interests are comparable, although children with ADHD may tend to migrate toward children of other ages.)

- Freedom from television.

Parents should not be paying for television as childcare. If television is present in a childcare setting, programs should be carefully selected for intrinsic value and freedom from aggression and tension. That means no Looney Tunes or Super Heroes, while Mr. Wizard, Care Bears and Sesame Street are winners.

Children with ADHD are drawn to television, because the constantly changing screen does not require them to sustain attention on any single thing. But they are particularly vulnerable to the more intense feelings it may stir. They are also very prone to copying in real life the aggressive actions they have viewed on television.

Some schools are working with community service agencies to provide formal social skills training programs as well as tutoring within the setting of after-school care programs on school grounds. This model offers the opportunity for maximum carry-over and communication about both social skills and academic issues.

Between Home and School

The section on Organization in Chapter 6 includes a discussion of a homework folder with a "To Home" pocket in the back and a "To School" pocket in the front as well as a central area for the homework assignment pages. Parents should check the folder and sign off when all assignments are done.

Students with ADHD should do their homework in the afternoon while their medication is still working and before they're distracted by dinner preparation and other evening activities. After a short (perhaps half an hour) break for food and exercise, the "homework supervisor" should sit down with the student to make a homework plan for the day.

Have the student estimate how long she or he needs for each assignment and tell you the preferred order. Make a list. Stack the needed books in the order of the list.

Get everything out of the bookbag, including lunch leftovers, messages home, and any papers that didn't get turned in on time. (If the subjects are color coded, this is easier—see the section on Organization in Chapter 6). Make sure that any assignments that extend over several days are distributed over the intervening time, with some allowance for an occasional skip day.

Use a timer or an alarm that measures small time increments, and set it for the time needed for the first task. When that task is accurately done, the student puts it in the To School pocket of the homework folder, returns the book to the bookbag, and checks off the list with a statement of self-congratulation.

This is followed by a brief exercise period (jogging in place, sit-ups, jumping rope) before moving on to the next assignment. Assignments that take more than ten or fifteen minutes should be divided into two sittings.

Procrastination, arguments and tears may prolong homework endlessly, needlessly. Find out from the teacher the amount of time appropriate for homework for the class. Increase that time by 30 to 45 minutes to allow for corrections, explanations and exercise breaks.

I Can't Sit Still

Make sure that amount of time is provided in a comfortable setting, where the child is protected from distraction by television, siblings, playmates and toys. (After-school activities may divide homework into two sections.) Then set an outer limit of time, perhaps 5 or 6 p.m. on days with after-school activities, and don't allow homework to go beyond that time.

The message needs to be very clear. If homework is done within that time period, the child is rewarded by enjoying a later activity (a bike ride, a walk, playing catch or a game with a parent, a special television program or time to play with a friend). If it is not completed in time, the child will receive the teacher's consequences at school and will not be allowed the reward activity.

Beyond that, it is "case closed." No nagging. Incomplete homework should not be allowed to contaminate the entire family interaction or to interfere with the important family "cozy time" enroute to bed.

Accuracy is a topic worth consideration for children with ADHD. They often have a strong tendency to just put down any old thing. This cheats the learning process and reinforces a bad habit. Children need a clear statement of acceptable lower limits of accuracy. An adult may need to check for accuracy before an assignment is signed off as done.

Using a Tutor

Children with ADHD may require considerable supervision to complete their homework. In addition to assistance with planning and checking, they may need an ongoing presence to keep them on task, particularly if medication is not used or has worn off. If the child tends to be oppositional, the added stress to family relationships may be too negative.

A high school or college student, learning center or after-school childcare person may be much more successful at helping with homework than a family member. Family energies can then be used for nurturing, sharing and relaxing. The homework supervisor should be given clear guidelines such as those included here and advised that challenges may lie ahead.

On the other hand, elementary children are often very eager to impress older students, who may also be better at the trick of making homework fun. The mere presence of a high-school student concentrating on his or her own homework at the same table may give the younger child an adequate model and motivation.

Children whose inattention precludes them from absorbing much of what is presented in class may need more intensive daily tutoring to make sure that they understand the materials as the class progresses.

Students in one college dormitory set up a very successful afternoon tutoring service. Their lobby and common areas were set up as study centers, and parents at several nearby schools were invited to bring students for free one-hour sessions twice a week.

Cooperative Advocacy

It is important to team with school professionals, using strategies similar to those used for teaming with a child. Teachers as well as parents and children need to hear the words *thank you.*

If you find yourself upset by the school's involvement with your child, ask for a meeting with the teacher. Share information about ADHD (such as this book) to help the teacher understand your child's special struggles. Do some joint problem solving.

It is best to have two adults who represent the child at the meeting. Acknowledge the challenges faced by a teacher with thirty or so students of differing needs at the same time that you advocate for your own child.

The school's nurse and resource specialist teacher, the local Learning Disabilities Association and private specialists (educational therapists, physicians and psychologists knowledgeable about children with school challenges including ADHD) can help you identify needs and obtain appropriate services for your struggling child.

Life's Pleasures

The development of social skills and opportunities for social success are as important to self-esteem and life success as the development of academic skills. Play with other children, sports and recreational activities, trips and excursions, and the arts give children the chance to interact with others and enjoy themselves while establishing these important skills.

Friendship

Children with ADHD, like many young children, will do best at play with one other child, not necessarily their own age. When there are several children in a family, you may want to invite over one playmate for each child.

For a child who is having a great deal of difficulty, structure each social experience at home for guaranteed success. First, set a short time frame for the children to play. A half hour is a good amount to begin with. If children continue to play together until they are no longer getting along, not getting along will be the last thing their friends recall about the experience.

Choose activities that don't involve territoriality and ownership. I don't expect my friends to use the things in my purse or cupboards unless I choose to get them out, but we expect our children to open all their cupboards and drawers to their friends.

The problem for children with ADHD is that even toys they intended to share may become more appealing when they are in the hands of a friend. Try planning outdoor play in a park or a walk to buy a cup of hot chocolate or a doughnut. Or you may want to get matching sets of toys such as walkie talkies or twin dolls.

Distractible children are likely to want to change play activities every two minutes. You may need to let the visitor finish a game with you that was started with your child. Or make a rule that children must take turns choosing activities and can't change sooner than every five or ten minutes.

Sharing rules could include switching mutually desired toys after two minutes, by the clock, and removing any toy that triggers a fight. Such rules need to be immediately and calmly enforced.

If both children are involved in a dispute, do not ask who started it. Say, "You both need a rest," and send them to separate rooms for as many minutes as they are years old. If you see your child getting into difficulty, remember to ask him or her to come aside privately.

If the playmate takes offense at the actions of your child and asks to leave, do not interfere. That logical consequence will probably have more impact on your child's impulsive behavior when similar situations arise than five lectures from you.

Recreation

Recreation involves a wonderful opportunity for winning experiences. It provides the chance to do what comes naturally.

Group sports may be less enjoyable for the child with ADHD than individual sports such as swimming, biking, aikido, karate and tennis. Individual sports are more divergent, there is minimal requirement for attentive waiting, and they do not present the distraction of all the other players. A sport should not be chosen just because every other child is doing it and certainly not just because the parent likes the sport.

Family Trips

Family vacation tends to be a difficult endeavor in many families. It may be even more challenging with a child with ADHD. However, planning that considers the child's needs and inclinations can result in successful times.

Whether traveling by car, plane, train or bus, provide at least one pre-wrapped package per half hour. Short, age-appropriate books, pencil and paper, small sock puppets or stuffed animals, and new tapes provide ample entertainment. (Be sure to provide tape recorders with earphones if you wish peace and quiet.)

Don't let the children see their "trip entertainers" before the trip. The surprise is part of the fun.

Additional tips include:

- Either camp or stay and eat in establishments that welcome children and have opportunities for action and noise.
- Be cautious of prolonged stays with relatives who are not enthusiastic about boisterous or grumpy, impulsive, wonderful children.
- Take along the comforters—the important blanket, pillow, or stuffed animal—that are a part of feeling safe and cozy.

Nurturing Talent

Don't forget music, drama, dance, art and even science projects as leisure activities. Children with ADHD are likely to be creative despite some difficulty staying with any one project. Choose activities that allow them the freedom to explore the medium.

In drama, a program in which children make up their own dramatic interpretations of suggested themes, either on the spot or after a short collaboration, is much more appropriate than putting on a play, with all of the rehearsals and waiting time involved. Story-telling is wonderfully successful recreation for many verbal children with ADHD, although they need some assistance in remembering to tell the story in sequence.

Free-form drawing, cartooning, painting, finger-painting and working with clay may absorb these children's interest, as long as people are not too worried about the number of pieces of paper used or the requirement that the project "look right" (whatever that means). For the musically inclined, choir, orchestra and bands open a wonderful world of shared pleasure, which is particularly valuable for the child who has trouble socializing verbally.

Piano lessons allow one-on-one instruction. Such instruction also provides experience in touch, sound, sight and sequence together, a wonderful assist in helping a child relate to left/right, lower/higher and before/after sequences.

Parenting does not stop with the ABCDEF tools. Faith, family and friends are part of the fullness of personhood that we want to offer our children, whoever they are. Underlying and beyond all the techniques is the value-giving relationship of love. Do not forget to pause to enjoy your children. Do not forget that you are a model and guide for them on life's journey.

Appendix A

Studies on Self-Esteem and ADHD

Studies have indicated that children with ADHD symptoms often have a significant decrease in self-esteem by the early grade school years (Campbell, 1977). A study of teenagers (Stewart, 1973) found that about 40 percent of those with ADHD have low self-esteem, compared to less than 10 percent of those without ADHD.

Other studies indicate that treatment can benefit the self-esteem of children with ADHD. Self-esteem improved in children with ADHD who were treated for six months with methlyphenidate (Ritalin), according to a 1982 study by Cohen and Thompson.

In a more recent study, the self-esteem of ADHD children ages eight to twelve improved substantially with sixteen months of therapy. The therapy included demystification, medication, regular pediatric follow-up and referral for mental health and special education assistance as necessary (Kelly et al., 1989).

In a long-term follow-up study by Weiss and Hechtman (1987, p.254-256), adults with ADHD who had been treated with medication had higher self-esteem ratings than those who hadn't been treated. Those treated perceived their childhoods as more positive. There was no difference in self-esteem ratings between those with ADHD who had been treated and adults who had not had ADHD.

The impact of ADHD on parent-child and teacher-child interactions influences not only child but adult self-esteem. Russell Barkley (1990) reviewed a number of studies examining these interactions.

The child with ADHD tends to elicit negative and controlling behavior from adults. When a child is treated with stimulant medication, negative commands and disapproval decrease and supportive interactions and positive parent-child communication increase. Teacher and peer responses to the child with ADHD also improve when the child is on medication.

The parents, particularly mothers, of children with ADHD often have much lower self-esteem than mothers of non-affected children. These mothers feel more depression, self-blame and social isolation. This depression leads to resentful involvement, overreaction to some infractions and intermittent withdrawal, which have a very negative impact on child self-esteem.

Relatives and friends of the parents of these challenging children, not understanding the nature of ADHD, tend to be critical of their parenting, which isolates the parents and contributes to their self-esteem problems. School staff can help in this difficult situation. The parent as well as the child needs a friendly word of recognition when something goes well.

Needless to say, teachers may also find themselves in the same spot, feeling inadequate and guiltily aware of their anger with the challenging child. This anger may then be projected onto the parent with comments such as, "Why don't you do something about your child!"

Teachers and mothers tend to have more difficulty with children with ADHD than fathers do. Fathers may not perceive that the child has difficulty, while mother and teacher are struggling intensely.

This difference may relate in part to the difference in authoritative male assertiveness or less rigorous expectations by the father. (He's just a boy. He's just like I was.) It may also relate to typical role divisions. Mother and teacher are primarily involved in supervision of convergent tasks (getting ready for school, doing schoolwork and homework, doing chores), while the father is more likely involved in more divergent activities (going to the park, rough-housing).

One study found that biological parents of a child with ADHD were three times as likely to separate or divorce over an eight-year period compared to other couples without ADHD children. It is not clear how much of this is due to stress from the child and how much from biological ADHD residual in a parent.

Certainly, some of the marital discord arises from the differences in parenting experiences and expectations, which become exaggerated by the challenges of the child with ADHD. Criticism of the spouse's parenting skills is common among parents of children with ADHD.

The impact of marital discord on a child's self-esteem is suggested by the response of a 13 year old with ADHD and a stable parental relationship. When I asked him what was most important to his self-esteem, he responded, "That my parents aren't divorced."

Appendix B

What Else Could It Be?

Children may be inattentive, restless, agitated, irritable, and off-task for many reasons unrelated to ADHD, whether or not they also have ADHD. These "secondary challenges" may stem from medical problems including poor health habits, learning disabilities and emotional difficulties.

Systematic investigation and treatment of these possibilities is intrinsic to the complete care of a child suspected of having ADHD. In many cases, the treatment of identified secondary challenges corrects the symptoms, clarifying that the child does not have ADHD. In other cases, the remaining symptoms of ADHD are then more readily treated.

Medical Challenges

Nursing assessment of vision and hearing are required first steps in assessing any child having difficulty paying attention in class. Height and weight that are out of the normal pattern for the child's family may suggest nutritional or hormonal difficulties such as hypothyroidism.

Medications and Substance Abuse

Most people have experienced the groggy feeling caused by taking certain antihistamines found in common allergy and cold medications. These same medicines may make it harder for children to remember things and can make some children act "hyper."

Theophylline, helpful in the treatment of asthma, and phenobarbital, often used to treat seizure disorders in children, are notorious for causing sensitive children to be excitable and hyperactive. Some children may be behaviorally sensitive to medicine in liquid but not tablet form, suggesting difficulty with something in the liquid (perhaps the dye or alcohol).

Substance abuse is an important factor in the older child with ADHD-like symptoms. While children with ADHD are at higher risk than others for substance abuse, the onset of ADHD-like behavior in the teen or preteen years should raise the suspicion of substance abuse without ADHD.

Illness

Chronic illness is another important factor. Anyone who has experienced a severe toothache, headache or backache knows that it's hard to concentrate on anything else but the pain. You may feel lacking in "brain energy" when you have influenza.

Likewise, children with anemia, chronic inflammatory illnesses such as arthritis, dental disease, or recurrent or chronic infections may be "out of it" when ill. Seizures can cause electrical "absence"; motor control disorders can cause involuntary movements; and pinworms can cause distracting itchiness.

Allergies are common. Constant nasal congestion, itchiness, annoying secretions and breathing difficulties, as well as the side-effects of medications, may be distracting. One important chronic problem sometimes associated with allergies is nighttime intermittent obstruction of the upper airway.

This problem, caused by swollen tonsils and adenoids, is associated with snoring and irregular breathing. Affected children may be chronically sleepy despite long hours in bed. If the large tonsils and adenoids do not shrink adequately with allergy management, such children may do much better if the tonsils or adenoids are removed.

Health Habits

A hungry, sleepy child cannot concentrate. Such a child may fidget, seem careless and be emotionally labile. A chronically malnourished or sleep-deprived child will have chronic symptoms similar to ADHD.

Special diets have not been found to be of value for most children with primary ADHD, but there are four aspects of diet that do relate to attention.

1. Deficits in basic nutrients compromise brain function in anyone. A healthy balanced diet is important.
2. A few children with ADHD do seem to be sensitive to particular food components, such as a dye, a preservative, chocolate or (in some preschoolers) sugar. When a child clearly reacts negatively to a particular food, avoid it if it does not complicate life for you or the child. But note that a dye or chocolate is more likely to cause the problem than sugar.
3. Studies by C. Keith Conners (1990) indicate that eating protein foods at breakfast (eggs, peanut butter, cheese, yogurt, milk, lunch meat, left-over pizza or chicken) helps children with ADHD concentrate. The effect is probably due to tyrosine, a chemical contained in protein. The neurotransmitters norepinephrine and dopamine are made from this chemical. Check the school breakfast menu, and have some peanut butter available for non-milk drinkers.

I Can't Sit Still

4. A child who has a true food allergy or sensitivity may develop an itchy mouth, runny nose or rash when eating that food—clearly not good for attention. The child may experience wheezing and swelling of the airway, which could be dangerous.

Sleep problems can be confusing. Lack of bedtime guidance or opportunity for quiet can cause symptoms due to sleeplessness that look like (but aren't) ADHD. However, children who do have ADHD are often very poor sleepers because of difficulty with their sleep-arousal-alerting mechanism.

Learning Disabilities and Related Problems

Learning disabilities and mental retardation often occur with ADHD, but they can also lead you to suspect ADHD when it isn't present. The retarded child may be globally immature in attention as well as motor and cognitive (thinking) abilities. (A child who does have ADHD and mental retardation may become more attentive and less impulsive, although not brighter, on medication.)

Children with auditory processing difficulties will tire of paying attention to language at a normal rate and complexity, as you would tire of paying attention to someone lecturing to you in a difficult, heavy accent.

Children who have visual-motor dissociation and cannot make a translation from visual perception to motor copy will not spend time focusing visually as they work, any more than you would look at your mirror image to write. (Try it!)

Children with sequencing problems tend to be disorganized and have trouble following sequential directions, problems also seen in children with ADHD.

ADHD symptoms may also occur with a number of conditions that have a medical or biological basis and associated learning, mood and socialization difficulties. Tourette's syndrome is associated with chronic tics, which may not appear until after the ADHD symptoms. Autism, Fragile X, Asperger syndrome and other conditions with symptoms of "pervasive developmental disorder" are characterized by atypical interpersonal interactions and language patterns. These children may have ADHD-like symptoms that in some cases respond to medication.

Emotional Factors

Emotional causes of secondary inattention may result from internal or environmental difficulties. Some children are biologically anxious or depressed, and therefore are edgy and don't pay attention. Children with underlying depression or anxiety are more likely than adults to be restless and aggressive.

Chronic embarrassment and failure are important considerations in the depressed, anxious, irritable, withdrawn child. In the classroom, a student is constantly being judged by peers as well as teacher.

Taunting from peers, recurrent criticism, innate sensitivity, learning challenges and significant difficulties in child-parent or child-teacher fit may contribute to secondary depression. Needless to say, the child who does have ADHD may also become depressed because of chronic failure and embarrassment.

Other children become anxious, depressed or aggressive because of parental depression, child abuse or spouse abuse, parental substance abuse, or frequent changes in household or caretaker. It is important to be alert to family chaos and initiate appropriate intervention.

It is also important to realize that ADHD is not ruled out by the presence of such circumstances. Remember that two major causes of ADHD are familial ADHD (which means one of the parents may have ADHD with resultant coping difficulties) and prenatal alcohol exposure (meaning that maternal alcoholism may be present). The presence of ADHD in a child may exaggerate problems in family interaction and parental depression and anger.

Television

Excessive television viewing has been identified as a cause of excessive aggression in children (Gadow, 1989). It has also been said to interfere with the development of the ability to keep paying attention to things.

On the other hand, parents of children with ADHD often report that their child can watch TV for hours. (This TV time may represent the parents' only relief from the constant need for supervision.)

This may seem strange. However, television is characterized by constant change in scene, action and sound, so there is no requirement to wait for the next thing to happen. Television viewing should be carefully monitored for all children, particularly aggressive children, whether or not they have ADHD.

Expectations

At times, a family or teacher suspects ADHD in a child who is simply manifesting age-appropriate impulsivity and inattention. This tertiary attentional difficulty is not really a difficulty within the child at all, but in the expectations adults may have of the child. In a noisy classroom, only the remarkably attentive can keep paying attention.

A third-grade teacher who teaches kindergarten for the first time may have difficulty adjusting his or her sense of "normal" to match the age of the students. This teacher may consider many normal children to be too hyperactive, inattentive and impulsive.

Children who are very tall for their age may be expected to have the attention span and impulse control to match their height rather than their age. Parents, teachers and caregivers should always ask themselves if their expectations are appropriate for any given child.

Appendix C

The School Assessment

The School, the Law and ADHD

A Policy Memorandum clarifying public schools' responsibilities to children with ADD was published on September 16, 1991, by the U.S. Department of Education.* It states that attention deficit disorder (with or without hyperactive disorder) falls within the existing federal laws regarding "children with disabilities," and that public schools are responsible for providing needed services accordingly to ensure these children a "free and appropriate education," even in the absence of other learning, emotional or physical disabilities.

The memorandum states that under the Individuals with Disabilities Education Act (IDEA—the updated version of Public Law 94-142), Part B (other health impaired), public schools have "an affirmative obligation" to the **identification** and **expeditious assessment** of students with ADD where it is suspected that the limitation in "alertness" (attention) puts them in need of special education and related services, "regardless of the severity of their disability."

The memorandum further states that "children with ADD should be classified as **eligible for services** under the 'other health impaired' category in instances where the ADD is a chronic or acute health problem that results in limited alertness, which adversely affects educational performance."

Individual evaluation of educational needs (IEP) involving a multidisciplinary staff with **at least one staff member knowledgeable about ADD** is required, even if medical diagnosis has been made. Only with school assessment can service eligibility and placement be determined, using the same criteria of need which would be applied for specific learning disabilities.

* "Clarification of Policy to Address the Needs of Children with ADD Within General and/or Special Education." September 16, 1991. United States Department of Education, Office of Special Education and Rehabilitative Services, 400 Maryland Ave. SW, Washington, DC 20202-2300.

Parents have the right of a due process hearing if a school refuses assessment or determines that the child is not eligible for services. The schools are responsible to provide **appropriate intervention for each separate disability** (learning disability, attention deficit, or serious emotional disturbance) which the child may have.

Students with ADD who are not eligible for services under Part B of the special education legislation may be eligible under the non-discrimination Section 504 of Federal Law 93-112, the Rehabilitation Act of 1973. Under Section 504, no one can be "excluded from participation in, be denied the benefits of, or be subjected to discrimination under any program or activity receiving federal financial assistance" solely on the basis of a handicap. A handicapped person is "any person who has a physical or mental **impairment which substantially limits** one or more of such person's major life activities"—including learning.

The Memorandum states that students with ADD who qualify for Section 504 services may require **modifications** in regular classroom structure, instructions and teaching technique; behavioral management; study aids; texts and workbooks; tests and nonacademic programs; as well as one-on-one tutoring, classroom aid or services coordination.

To receive a full copy of the memorandum, call the Offices of Civil Rights, (202) 732-1635, Special Education Programs (202) 732-1007, or Elementary and Secondary Education (202) 401-0984.

ADHD Symptoms and IEP Testing

When ADHD is suspected, the school psychologist or educational specialist needs to:
- clarify the child's actual intellectual ability and areas of strength
- identify possible learning disabilities
- compare achievement testing when alone with the student to group achievement testing, classroom performance and aptitude.

As many as 40 percent of children with ADHD have associated learning disabilities. Likewise, mental retardation or a learning disability may cause children to demonstrate some of the symptoms of ADHD in their weak content areas.

Testers should compare their testing observations with work samples to see how much the one-on-one special situation of testing affects work quality. Some students with ADHD can do well in the low-distraction office of a tester who helps them stay on task but are unable to stay on task in the classroom.

There's no one test that's perfect for identifying ADHD. Different students demonstrate differing symptoms, and inconsistent performance is one of the more reliable aspects of ADHD.

The psychologist or education specialist will gather important data from testing observations as well as results. The pattern that emerges from "how" the student takes the test and the reasons for the errors may be as significant as the errors themselves.

Some creative testing may be required to see if performance changes when circumstances or techniques change. The academic error patterns a teacher observes in reading, writing, spelling and math may also be evident on psychological testing.

Loose steering problems of inattention are evidenced with distractibility, attentional fatigue and omission errors during testing. Distractibility is indicated if performance drops suddenly when there is a noise outside, or if the child does better on a listening task if his or her eyes are closed.

Attentional fatigue is evident when performance declines over a series of tasks of the same difficulty level, when there is deterioration in performance over the total time of testing, or when yawning, resting the head on the table and other signs of exhaustion appear. Omission errors may be the result of disorganized approach so that patterns are skipped, of superficial attention associated with impulsivity, or of the fatigue of "burn-out."

Inconsistent performance may be a reflection of both inattention and impulsivity. It may be seen when a student does better on some difficult tasks than on other similar tasks which are comparable or easier. Sometimes the use of excited voice tones, opportunity for exercise or rest, or use of rewards such as stickers significantly improves attentional focus.

A task requiring sustained focus may be started with great care and reflection, only to deteriorate in a burst of haste. Performance rate may vary from pauses associated with off-task activity or daydreaming to extreme haste, and perhaps "stuckness" (perseveration) as the child insists on completing something even though time is up for that task.

Speed spurts or impulse-control problems are evidenced in starting before instructions have been completed and making errors with fast responses that are corrected afterward (with or without instruction). The imposition of focus and reflection (Don't answer yet. Look more carefully. Think before you respond.) may improve performance.

Commission errors are seen on tests specifically designed to see how well a student can choose only the correct patterns. These are a particularly sensitive indicator of impulsivity.

Specific Tests

On the Wechsler Intelligence Scale for Children—Revised (WISC-R), perhaps the most commonly used intelligence test for school-age children, the average of scores on the Arithmetic, Coding and Digit Span have been called the "Freedom from Distractibility Factor." Those tests are generally felt to be particularly vulnerable to inattention and impulsivity. If there is no other reason for compromise of performance on those tests and the average scores on those tests are significantly lower than the average of scores on the other subtests, ADHD may be suspected.

The Kagan Matching Familiar Figures test tends to demonstrate rapid and inaccurate performance in children with ADHD, as they try to identify the two exactly identical figures of several that are different only in fine detail.

Vigilance tests are particularly specific for ADHD. These involve the student in a boring, repetitive search for sets matching a particular pattern. The Stroop Color-Word

Task, a checking task, and the Gordon Diagnostic are among commonly used vigilance tests that are scored for errors of omission (inattention) and commission (impulsivity).

Reaction of choice requires the student to show right hand to one tap and left hand to two taps. Conflict of reaction requires the hand to be raised high to a soft tap and low to a loud tap.

Rating scales filled out by parents and teachers help in determining whether a particular child has ADHD or other problems. One problem is that most of these scales describe only problems and no strengths. They do allow the views of a number of observers to be compared to each other and to population averages.

The Conners rating scales are commonly used because they are well standardized. They were designed as research tools for monitoring medication effects and are more sensitive to impulsivity than to inattention difficulties.

The items on the Yale Children's Inventory were developed from detailed histories of children with ADHD and some secondary problems. This inventory is an excellent parent scale for use by a school team initiating assistance for a child. It includes brief sections on depression, sleep, conduct disorder and learning difficulties, as well as attention, hyperactivity and impulsivity.

The Levine ANSER system includes fairly lengthy questionnaires for parents and teacher, as well as students age nine and older. While not well standardized, it helps one learn a lot about the child's strengths and looks quite closely at learning differences, anxiety and depression, as well as the child-troubling symptoms of ADHD.

School Nurse Role

At school, the medical aspects of the differential diagnosis of ADHD require at least a good vision and hearing examination; record of blood pressure and pulse, height and weight; and an exploration of health habits, medications and recognized illnesses. A complete medical history and exam are part of the assessment to check for medical causes of secondary attentional difficulties.

The school nurse may help organize school information for physician review, aid the family in locating a physician if they do not have one, and provide the translation of the physician report into the school setting. The nurse may also aid the family in completing a medical history form.

For physician referral, speak first with the family's physician. Generally, board-certified specialists in pediatrics, child neurology and child psychiatry are able to provide most extensive assistance.

The neurologist is most helpful if there are seizures, a significant movement disorder or retardation. The psychiatrist is of particular value when you suspect serious mood disturbance (depression, rage), thought disorder (hallucinations, paranoia) or conduct disorder (setting fires, stealing, drug abuse.) The developmental pediatrician is appropriate for the common combination of learning and behavioral problems.

Appendix D

Yale Children's Inventory *

Good questionaires are very helpful in the process of diagnosing a child's challenges. The Medical Data Base found in *Physician-School Collaboration for the Student with Attentional Difficulties: Handbook for Intervention* (Johnson, 1991), is a format for collecting medical and family information.

The Yale Children's Inventory presented here provides the important complementary information about learning, conduct and emotional challenges, as well as inattention. It is easily administered and analyzed, and is based on careful evaluation of a much longer questionaire completed for hundreds of children through the Yale Center for the Study of Learning and Attention Disorders.

Responses to the questionaire can guide the focus of further assessment and assistance. For example, if there are many 3's and 4's checked under Feelings, concerns about underlying depression would lead to mental health consultation. Likewise, high scores under Behavioral I and II would suggest the need for mental health assistance for child and family. If there are many 3's and 4's checked under Learning or Performing, testing for possible learning disabilities would be important. A diagnosis of ADHD would be more likely in a child who had 3's and 4's on most items under Attention, Impulsivity and Activity. The child with 1's and 2's on Impulsivity, Activity and Feelings but 3's and 4's on Attention may have attention deficit disorder without hyperactivity.

Child's name
_____

Today's date
_____

Child's birthdate
_____

Child's sex
_____

Below is a list of characteristics pertaining particularly to school and school work. From your experience working with this child, from information obtained in report cards or in conferences, indicate whether the characteristic is true: *Never, Rarely, Sometimes* or *Often*. It is *very important* that you answer *each* question, if you aren't sure, choose the response that seems closest to your impression.

Attention	Never	Rarely	Sometimes	Often
Confuses the details	1	2	3	4
Doesn't finish what she/he starts (a book, puzzle)	1	2	3	4
Needs a calm, quiet atmosphere in order to work or concentrate	1	2	3	4
Hears but doesn't seem to listen	1	2	3	4
Has difficulty concentrating or paying attention unless in one-on-one structured situation	1	2	3	4
Asks to have things repeated	1	2	3	4
Is easily distracted	1	2	3	4
Adaptability				
Does not adjust to new situations	1	2	3	4
Does not adapt to changes in routine	1	2	3	4
Has mood fluctuations usually unrelated to situation	1	2	3	4
Is slow to respond	1	2	3	4
Impulsivity				
Disrupts other children	1	2	3	4
Has trouble waiting his/her turn	1	2	3	4
Talks excessively	1	2	3	4
Calls out in class; makes noises in class	1	2	3	4
Is extremely excitable	1	2	3	4

Note: The following are lists of characteristic behaviors. Indicate which are *Never* true of this child or *Rarely, Sometimes* or *Often* true.

	Never	Rarely	Sometimes	Often
Activity				
For ages from *birth up to 6* years old:				
Climbed onto cabinets and furniture	1	2	3	4
Was always on the go; would run rather than walk	1	2	3	4
For ages *6 or older:*				
Fidgets or squirms	1	2	3	4
Does things in a loud and noisy way	1	2	3	4
Must always be doing something or she/he becomes fidgety	1	2	3	4
Manageability				
For ages from *birth up to 6* years old:				
Broke toys and other things; was destructive	1	2	3	4
Couldn't tolerate a noisy, busy place; would go wild in a crowd	1	2	3	4
Very difficult to take for a visit to friends	1	2	3	4
Very difficult to leave with a babysitter	1	2	3	4
Very difficult to take shopping	1	2	3	4
Needed constant supervision	1	2	3	4
Behavioral I				
At *any age,* this child:				
Must do things "my way"; can't be taught how to do things	1	2	3	4
Cheats; has to be the winner	1	2	3	4
Complains of unfair treatment; everyone is against him/her	1	2	3	4
Extends himself/herself only if it is an advantage to himself/ herself	1	2	3	4
Is a "sponger" (takes favors with no effort to return them)	1	2	3	4

Behavioral II

Did any of the following occur over an *extended period of time* (six months or more):	No	Yes
Swearing, use of vulgar language	1	2
Lying to other than family members	1	2
Was violent and aggressive, assaulted others, got into fights	1	2
Wants friends, but provokes them to anger	1	2

This child: (Circle only *one* response):	
Never steals or breaks rules	1
Will only steal or break rules if she/he thinks no one is around	2
May even steal or break rules when she/he is supervised	3
Even steals or breaks rules while she/he is closely supervised	4

Feelings

Note: During ages *2-1/2 - 5* how did this child interact with other children? Indicate on the following list if the characteristic is true of this child *Never, Rarely, Sometimes* or *Often.*

This child:	Never	Rarely	Sometimes	Often
Wants friends but is rejected or avoided by other children	1	2	3	4
Gets feelings hurt easily by children	1	2	3	4

Note: For *ages 6 or older.*	Never	Rarely	Sometimes	Often
Has been depressed, sad, down in the dumps	1	2	3	4
Cries for slightest reason	1	2	3	4
Has been pessimistic; always thinks things will go badly	1	2	3	4
Has had a poor self-image; feels worthless	1	2	3	4

I Can't Sit Still

Note: Indicate how difficult or easy the following activities were for this child to learn and how well she/he performs them now. If the skill was never attempted for whatever reason (handicap, child is too young) check *Not Applicable.*

	Learning				Performing				
	Easy	Not Too Difficult	Pretty Difficult	Very Difficult	Very Well	Pretty Well	Not Too Well	Poor or Unable	Not Applicable
Academic									
Activity:									
Tell time	1	2	3	4	1	2	3	4	99
Count money	1	2	3	4	1	2	3	4	99
Recognize numbers	1	2	3	4	1	2	3	4	99
Recognize letters	1	2	3	4	1	2	3	4	99
Fine Motor									
Activity:									
Eat with utensils	1	2	3	4	1	2	3	4	99
Get dressed by himself/herself	1	2	3	4	1	2	3	4	99
Do buttons and zippers	1	2	3	4	1	2	3	4	99
Tie shoes	1	2	3	4	1	2	3	4	99
Draw	1	2	3	4	1	2	3	4	99
Fine hand work in general, such as puzzles, models	1	2	3	4	1	2	3	4	99

Note: The following are lists of characteristics of speech. For the two age groups indicate whether the characteristic is *Never True* or *Sometimes, Often,* or *Almost Always True.*

Language	Never	Sometimes	Often	Almost Always
During ages *2-1/2 - 5* did this child:				
Hesitate or stop mid sentence	1	2	3	4
Seem to understand but have trouble getting the words out	1	2	3	4
Have difficulty finding the right word	1	2	3	4
Confuse the order of words, such as "Ball, I hit"	1	2	3	4
Unable to tell about what happened to him/her (such as about his/her day)	1	2	3	4
During ages *6 and over:*				
Confuse words that sound alike, such as hem/hen	1	2	3	4
Have trouble pronouncing words	1	2	3	4

I Can't Sit Still

Appendix E

Diagnostic Criteria

Diagnostic Criteria for 314.01
Attention-Deficit Hyperactivity Disorder*

Note: Consider a criterion met only if the behavior is considerably more frequent than that of most people of the same mental age.

A. A disturbance of at least six months during which at least eight of the following are present:

(1) often fidgets with hands or feet or squirms in seat (in adolescents, may be limited to subjective feelings of restlessness)

(2) has difficulty remaining seated when required to do so

(3) is easily distracted by extraneous stimuli

(4) has difficulty awaiting turn in games or group situations

(5) often blurts out answers to questions before they have been completed

(6) has difficulty following through on instructions from others (not due to oppositional behavior or failure of comprehension), e.g., fails to finish chores

(7) has difficulty sustaining attention in tasks or play activities

(8) often shifts from one uncompleted activity to another

(9) has difficulty playing quietly

(10) often talks excessively

(11) often interrupts or intrudes on others, e.g., butts into other children's games

(12) often does not seem to listen to what is being said to him or her

---

* Reprinted with permission from the American Psychiatric Association: *Diagnostic and Statistical Manual of Mental Disorders, Third Edition, Revised.* Washington, D.C.: American Psychiatric Association, 1987.

(13) often loses things necessary for tasks or activities at school or at home, e.g., toys, pencils, books, assignments

(14) often engages in physically dangerous activities without considering possible consequences (not for the purpose of thrill-seeking), e.g., runs into street without looking

Note: The above items are listed in descending order of discriminating power based on data from a national field trial of the DSM-III-R criteria for Disruptive Behavior Disorders.

B. Onset before the age of seven.

C. Does not meet the criteria for a Pervasive Developmental Disorder.

Criteria for Severity of Attention-Deficit Hyperactivity Disorder

Mild: Few, if any, symptoms in excess of those required to make the diagnosis and only minimal or no impairment in school and social functioning.

Moderate: Symptoms or functional impairment intermediate between "mild" and "severe."

Severe: Many symptoms in excess of those required to make the diagnosis and significant and pervasive impairment in functioning at home and school and with peers.

Appendix F

More About Medication

Medications commonly used for ADHD are the stimulants, Ritalin (methylphenidate), Dexedrine (dextroamphetamine) and Cylert (pemoline.) Tofranil (imipramine) and Norpramine (desipramine) are tricyclic antidepressants that can help some students with ADHD. Catapres (clonidine) is a drug more recently being used for children with Tourette's syndrome, which seems to benefit some children with ADHD, particularly those who tend to be more active and aggressive, but does not seem to improve attention per se.

Common Concerns

Side effects of the stimulants are usually mild. More than three decades of use have shown these medications to be remarkably safe, both short- and long-term, when moderate doses are used. The exception is a potentially serious sensitivity reaction to Cylert, which affects the liver in approximately 1 percent of children receiving it.

Liver functions should be checked prior to treatment with Cylert, a month later, and approximately every four months subsequently so the medication can be stopped promptly if a reaction occurs. Fortunately, the liver function returns to normal in most patients once the medication is stopped.

The development of an allergic rash, which goes away when the medication is stopped, is occasionally reported with stimulants, but it is not associated with toxicity.

With all stimulants, children may experience loss of appetite during the time when the medication is effective, so don't nag about lunch, but do make sure they have a good breakfast and dinner. Long-term growth does not appear to be significantly affected by the medication, though in the first months there may be some minor weight loss and height slowing.

Other side effects are seen in some children. Some children may have difficulty sleeping when medication is first used. Sleep difficulties may continue with the use of Cylert, which may be effective as long as 14 hours. They occur less frequently with the Dexedrine Spansule, a long-acting capsule preparation, which improves concentration for about ten hours.

Sleep difficulties may also occur when other stimulants are given late in the day. Associated headaches and stomach aches are usually mild, and stomach aches are less common if the medication is given with food.

Tics, repetitive involuntary movements, develop in approximately 1 percent of children with ADHD who are treated with stimulants. Tics will resolve after stopping medication in 98 percent of children who develop them (Gadow and Sverd, 1990).

However, children with Tourette's syndrome, a chronic tic disorder, may display ADHD symptoms before the tics develop. In such children, the medication may "unmask" or even decrease rather than cause the tics.

Mood changes are probably the most frustrating potential side effect of medication. Rebound, increased moodiness as medication is wearing off, is particularly common with the short-acting stimulants. It can usually be addressed by using the full dose of medication in the morning, followed by two progressively smaller doses later.

Ritalin, for example, may be prescribed as 10 mg at 8 a.m., 7.5 mg at noon, and 5 mg around 3 p.m., moving the third dose early enough to allow for evening appetite and sleep. (The actual doses depend on the individual child's weight and medication effect.)

Some children feel very weepy, irritable, grumpy or anxious on the medication. These difficult moods (dysphoria) may go away after the first weeks on medication. If the moods persist, the dosage can be adjusted or the medication can be changed.

The anxious response to stimulant medication is most likely to occur in those children who were already anxious. Increased lip biting, lip licking and finger picking may occur on higher doses.

In some students, the medication seems to have an excessively "sobering" effect—the child may seem too serious and tense. Fortunately, children who experience mood difficulties on one medication can often take another without difficulty. Generally, such difficulties are less likely to develop on lower doses of medication.

Excessively high doses of medication may result in psychotic symptoms, which stop when the medication is stopped. Stimulants should not be used in children with preexisting psychosis or thought disorder (Barkley, 1990).

Many people are concerned that the prescription use of medication to treat ADHD symptoms may predispose a child to later drug or alcohol abuse. As a population, young people with ADHD are more likely to be involved in substance abuse than their peers who do not have ADHD. Their impulsivity and low self-esteem get in the way of "just saying no."

However, Weiss and Hechtman (1987, p. 283) have found that students with ADHD are less likely to abuse alcohol or drugs when they are appropriately treated, and they do not abuse their own medication.

The decision to prescribe medication for a child should be made with reserve and caution. Most importantly, it should be made only after careful assessment and with the guidance of a physician knowledgeable about appropriate dosing since most of the problematic side effects are dose related. It is also important that the physician can communicate effectively with the child as well as the parents.

School personnel can guide families to seek skilled professional assistance for their child, but they should not push the use of medication per se. Parents and teachers must realize that medication cannot be safely pushed to levels high enough to resolve all of the child's symptoms of ADHD. That's why the rest of this book is important, whether or not a child is on medication.

Sustaining Medication

Careful literature review and long-term research studies by Weiss and Hechtman, as well as Rachel Gittleman Klein (1987) indicate that medication continues to be effective for symptoms of ADHD throughout adolescence. Prior suggestions that ADHD is always outgrown and medication ineffective in teenagers have been found to be inaccurate.

Regular medical monitoring is imperative during treatment. Episodic trials off medication can verify that it is still needed. If a child does reasonably well socially off medication, medication can be stopped during vacations.

Some children tolerate being off medication on weekends as well, while others seem to experience more side effects the early part of each week after their weekends off. Children who have serious peer and family interaction difficulties that are improved on medication should continue on medication, except for a yearly trial period to verify that the medication is still required.

Generic or Brand Name?

Brand-name medications are more reliable in the concentration of medication they contain, but generally are more expensive. If symptoms seem to increase in severity with the change to a generic form of a medication, speak with the physician. It's possible that only brand-name medication should be used.

Suggested Readings

Archer, A. and M. Gleason. 1989. *Skills for School Success*. North Billerica, MA: Curriculum Associates.

Bash, M.A. and B. Camp. 1985. *Think Aloud: A Problem-Solving Program for Children*. Champaign, IL: Research Press.

Bodenhamer, G. 1987. *Back In Control: How to Get Your Children to Behave*. New York: Prentice Hall.

Clark, L. 1989. *The Time-Out Solution*. Chicago: Contemporary Books.

Curwin, R.L. and A.N. Mendler. 1990. *Am I in Trouble? Using Discipline to Teach Young Children Responsibility*. Santa Cruz, CA: ETR Associates.

Faber, A. and E. Mazlish. 1987. *Siblings Without Rivalry*. New York: Hearst Books.

Harris, S. and N. Brower. 1988. *The Good Behavior Book and Board*. Fountain Valley, CA: Behavior Products.

Levine, M. 1990. *Keeping a Head in School*. Cambridge, MA: Educators Publishing Service.

Kendall, P.C. 1988. *Stop and Think Workbook*. Merion Station, PA.

McGinnis, E. and A. Goldstein. 1990. *Skill Streaming in Early Childhood: Teaching Prosocial Skills to the Preschool and Kindergarten Child*. Champaign, IL: Research Press.

McGinnis, E. and A. Goldstein with R.P. Spratkin and N.J. Gershaw. 1984. *Skill Streaming the Elementary School Child: A Guide to Teaching Prosocial Skills*. Champaign, IL: Research Press.

Mendler, A.N. 1990. *Smiling at Yourself: Educating Young Children About Stress and Self-Esteem*. Santa Cruz, CA: ETR Associates.

References

Archer, A. and M. Gleason. 1989. *Skills for school success.* North Billerica, MA: Curriculum Associates.

Barkley, R.A. 1990. *Attention deficit hyperactivity disorder: A handbook for diagnosis and treatment.* New York: Guilford Press.

Bash, M.A. and B. Camp. 1985. *Think aloud: A problem-solving program for children.* Champaign, IL: Research Press.

Campbell, S.B., M.W. Endman and G. Bernfeld. 1977. A three-year follow-up of hyperactive preschoolers into elementary school. *Journal of Child Psychology and Psychiatry* 18:239-249.

Cohen, N.J., J. Sullivan, K. Minde, C. Novak and S. Keene. 1983. Mother-child interaction in hyperactive and normal kindergarten-aged children and the effect of treatment. *Child Psychiatry and Human Development* 13:213-224.

Cohen, N.J. and L. Thompson. 1982. Perceptions and attitudes of hyperactive children and their mothers regarding treatment with methylphenidate. *Canadian Journal of Psychiatry* 27:40-42.

Conners, C.K. 1990. Paper presented at the Learning Disabilities Association of America International Conference, February 21-24, Anaheim, CA.

Douglas, V.I., R.G. Barr, K. Amin, M.E. O'Neill and B. G. Britton. 1988. Dosage effects and individual responsivity to methylphenidate in attention deficit disorder. *Journal of Child Psychology and Psychiatry* 29 (4): 453-475.

Gadow, K.D., E.E. Nolan, J. Sverd, J. Sprafkin and L. Paolicelli. 1990. Methylphenidate in aggressive-hyperactive boys: I. Effects on peer aggression in public school settings. *Journal of the American Academy of Child Adolescent Psychiatry* 29:710.

Gadow, K.D. and J. Sverd. 1990. Stimulants for ADHD in child patients with Tourette's syndrome: The issue of relative risk. *Journal of Development Behavior Pediatrics* 11:269-271.

Gadow, K.D. and J. Sprafkin. 1989. Field experiments of television violence with children: Evidence for an environmental hazard? *Pediatrics* 83:399-405.

Johnson, D. D. 1991. Physician–school collaboration for the student with attentional difficulties: Handbook for intervention. San Diego: Author.

Klein, R.G. 1987. Prognosis of attention deficit disorder and its management in adolescence. *Pediatrics in Review* 8 (7): 216-222.

Stewart, M.A., W.B. Mendelson and N.E. Johnson. 1973. Hyperactive children as adolescents: How they describe themselves. *Child Psychiatry and Human Development* 4:3-11.

Weiss, G. and L. Hechtman. 1987. *Hyperactive children grown up.* New York: Guilford Press.

Zametkin, A., T. Nordahl, M. Gross, A.C. King, W.E. Semple, J. Rumsey, S. Hamburger and R. Cohen. 1990. Cerebral glucose metabolism in adults with hyperactivity of childhood onset. *The New England Journal of Medicine* 323:20.

About the Author

Dorothy Davies Johnson, MD, FAAP, is a graduate of the Pritzker School of Medicine, University of Chicago. She completed her pediatric residency at the University of Rochester, New York, where she participated in a model school health program. She served on the faculty of the Department of Pediatrics at the University of California, San Diego, from 1974 until 1981, when she entered private practice in general pediatrics.

Dr. Johnson has had long-term involvement with the schools, providing inservice training to nurses, therapists and teachers and reviewing student needs for therapy services. She currently serves as chair of the School Health Committee for the local chapter of the American Academy of Pediatrics. Her sub-specialty training in developmental pediatrics focused on learning and attentional challenges of the school-age child.

Now a full-time private consultant in developmental pediatrics, Dr. Johnson assesses and cares for challenged children in a multidisciplinary therapeutic setting. She is pediatric consultant to Partners for Attentionally Related Disorders (PARD) in the San Diego Unified School District, funded by a grant from the American Academy of Pediatrics and Maternal and Child Health. In 1989, she received the first Community Leader Award from the San Diego chapter of the California Association of Resource Specialists.

Dr. Johnson has participated in conferences throughout the United States, including conferences sponsored by the American School Health Association, San Diego Children's Hospital and Health Center, and the Learning Disabilities Association of Nebraska. She is the author of *Physician-School Collaboration for Children with Attentional Difficulties: Handbook for Intervention,* a version of which is on each elementary school campus participating in the PARD project.

Tackle Today's Tough Issues
With More Practical Handbooks

Positively Different
Creating a Bias-Free Environment for Young Children

Ana Consuelo Matiella, MA

(#509-H1)

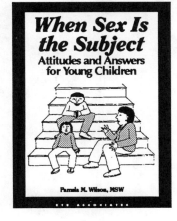

When Sex Is the Subject
Attitudes and Answers for Young Children

Pamela M. Wilson, MSW

(#583-H1)

Am I Fat?
Helping Young Children Accept Differences in Body Size

Joanne Ikeda, MA, RD
Priscilla Naworski, MS, CHES

(#569-H1)

I Can't Sit Still
Educating and Affirming Inattentive and Hyperactive Children

Dorothy Davies Johnson, MD, FAAP

(#560-H1)

Handle with Care
Helping Children Prenatally Exposed to Drugs and Alcohol

Sylvia Fernandez Villarreal, MD
Lora-Ellen McKinney, PhD
Marcia Quackenbush, MS, MFCC

(#594-H1)

Learn a variety of positive, hands-on approaches to help children up to age ten understand the health issues that shape their lives. The Issues Books from ETR Associates. For more information and a complete list of Issues Books...

Call Toll-Free 1 (800) 321-4407

or contact:
Sales Department
ETR Associates
P.O. Box 1830
Santa Cruz, CA 95061-1830
FAX: (408) 438-4284